Past-into-Present Series

HOLIDAYS

Sheila Gordon
*Department of History,
Kingsdale Comprehensive School, Dulwich*

B. T. BATSFORD LTD   London

First published 1972
© Sheila Gordon, 1972

Filmset by Keyspools Ltd, Golborne, Lancs.

Printed in Great Britain by The Anchor Press, Tiptree, Essex
for the Publishers

B. T. Batsford Ltd, 4 Fitzhardinge Street, London W1H OAH

ISBN 0 7134 1780 3

Contents

Acknowledgments   4
List of Illustrations   5
  1 High Days and Holidays   7
  2 To Go on Pilgrimages   18
  3 Waddling to the Waters   29
  4 The Discovery of the Coast   40
  5 I Do Like to be beside the Sea   51
  6 In Search of Beauty   65
  7 Between the Wars   76
  8 Holidays Today   86
Further Reading   94
Index   95

Acknowledgment

The Author and Publisher would like to thank the following for the illustrations appearing in this book: the British Museum for figs. 13 and 14; the British Museum of Transport for fig. 52; BOAC for fig. 59; British Railways for fig. 37; British Transport Hotels Ltd. for fig. 49; Butlin's Ltd. for fig. 56; the Camping Club for fig. 61; the Central Council for Physical Recreation for figs. 63 (*Yorkshire Post*) and 64 (*Sunderland Echo*); Thomas Cook Ltd. for figs. 44, 46 and 47; the French Government Tourist Office for fig. 45; the London Museum for figs. 6, 12, 30 and 65; the Ministry of Works for fig. 8; Radio Times Hulton Picture Library for fig. 58; W. Scott for fig. 9; the Scottish Tourist Board for fig. 60; the Tate Gallery for figs. 28, 40 and 43; the Victoria and Albert Museum for figs. 5, 22, 32, 33, 35, 41, 48, 50 and 51; Weymouth Public Library for fig. 23; the Youth Hostels Association (G. Tatlock) for fig. 62.
Fig. 42 is reproduced by gracious permission of Her Majesty the Queen.

The Illustrations

1	Slaying animals	7
2	Mediaeval peasants harvesting	9
3	Mummers at a feast	12
4	Jousting	14
5	Hunting	15
6	A Tudor holy day	16
7	A Victorian Christmas	16
8	Avebury stones	18
9	Glastonbury	19
10	Pilgrims at Canterbury	21
11	Pilgrims on a journey	23
12	Badges collected by pilgrims	25
13	Animals of the Holy Land	26
14	Jerusalem	27
15	Taking the mineral waters	29
16	Tunbridge Wells,	30
17	Bathing at Bath	32
18	Beau Nash	33
19	Cross Bath	34
20	Bath, morning gossip	35
21	A ball at the Assembly Rooms	36
22	St. Peter's, Rome	38
23	Sea dipping, Weymouth	41
24	Scarborough	42
25	The Steyne, Brighton	43
26	Margate packet	45
27	Weymouth	47
28	Chain pier, Brighton	48
29	Brighton Pavilion	48
30	Tottenham Court Road turnpike	50
31	A Toll Gate	51
32	Travelling carriage	52
33	Seaford	53
34	Bathing machine	55
35	Bathing on a rope	56
36	Victorian bathing fashions	57
37	Third-class railway travel	60
38	Seaside pier, 1895	62
39	Blackpool, 1895	63
40	*Gordale Scar*, by James Ward	65
41	An artist at the seaside	66
42	Queen Victoria in Scotland	67
43	*Bridge of Sighs*, by Turner	68
44	Nineteenth-century travellers, Switzerland	69
45	The Riviera	70
46	Thomas Cook party, Paris	71
47	Cook's Tours, 1885	72
48	Victorian house party	73
49	Gleneagles Hotel	74
50	On the beach	76
51	A travel poster	77
52	Waterloo Station, 1906	78
53	Poster for Skegness	80
54	Holiday Fellowship guest house	81
55	Boarding houses	83
56	Butlin's Holiday Camp, Skegness	84
57	A Middle East touring party	84
58	August Bank Holiday, 1944	86
59	*BOAC* poster	87
60	Skiers	89
61	Campers	90
62	A Youth Hostel	91
63	Pony trekking	92
64	Sailing	93
65	A traffic jam	93

1 High Days and Holidays

Ever since his remote beginnings, Man has had to work hard to stay alive; he has always therefore made the most of those times when work could be laid aside for a while. Even in the oldest, primitive societies, in which the struggle for survival was particularly harsh and unrelenting, there must have been times when a man was able to lie back in the firelight, enjoy his food and drink and watch his children at play. Yet primitive man never felt free for long to enjoy the delight of doing nothing. He was always aware that the gods were watching him. These were the powers on whom he believed his life depended. They controlled in some mysterious way the sun that ripened his crops; the rain and great rivers that irrigated his fields; the fertility that alone could ensure a good harvest and full stomachs for his children. These were not gods to be treated casually. They had to be placated with sacrifices, worshipped in elaborate rituals, and entertained with dancing and games. Whether he was a hunter or a farmer, he felt safer if he devoted his spare time to the rites celebrated in their honour. Moreover, he got more out of it all than reassurance; the necessity of keeping the gods happy meant that he got an occasional break from work even at the busiest times of the year. In primitive times a holy day was certainly a most welcome holiday.

It seemed obvious to primitive man that there were certain periods of the year when the gods were in special need of propitiation. These were times of ploughing, of sowing the corn, of its first springing from the ground, and of harvest. It also

1 December had always been a time when animals were killed, a time of feasting.

seemed to him that there were four days in the year which were quite unlike any other and must therefore be of great significance. These were the two days when daylight and dark were exactly equal – the summer and Autumn equinoxes – and the two days when they are at their most unequal – Midsummer and Midwinter. At these times primitive man organized his most important festivals – and when we think of their continuing place in our lives today, we may realize the strength of the links that still bind us to our ancestors.

Those basic human needs that the old gods were thought to take care of, are common to all men, and it is not surprising that we find gods and festivals whose names vary from one area to another, but which seem to have played similar roles in people's lives. Often gods worshipped by societies who lived hundreds, even thousands of miles apart, had extraordinary similarities. This came about sometimes, of course, because of migration from one place to another, but most often because the rights were rooted in similar problems and experiences, and in the same events of the farming year. However complex the rituals became as their followers moved away from a primitive pattern of existence, and grew more sophisticated, the old basic imperatives of seedtime and harvest remained, and so did the gods who presided over them.

Saturn and Freya
One of the most important festivals in the Roman year was 'Saturnalia' – the festival devoted to Saturn, the god of corn and fertility. Saturnalia came at Midwinter; it lasted from the nineteenth to the twenty-fourth of December and was a time of wild merry-making. The normal routine of life, the order and discipline on which Roman power depended, were forgotten, and for a brief period the world turned topsy-turvy. Masters feasted with slaves, sometimes even waited on them; schools were closed; punishments were forbidden and no battles were fought. Every house was decorated with garlands of evergreen, the symbols of life that would endure throughout the dark winter; candles were lit and little wax dolls were made as gifts for the children.

The Anglo Saxons were far removed from Roman civilisation not only by distance but by their more primitive way of life, and by their harsher environment. As they wrested a living from the sandy wastes and marshland of north Germany, and from the waters of the cold North Sea, they turned to gods who were fittingly cruel and warlike – who demanded from their followers not gentleness and compassion, but the toughness and courage that were needed to survive in an unfriendly land. Nevertheless, the Saxons were farmers as well as warriors, and at the heart of their religion just like that of the more sophisticated Romans, was the spirit of corn and fertility, whose name was not Saturn but Freya, a goddess found throughout the mythologies of Northern Europe. The Saxons, just like the Romans, observed their most important festival at Midwinter, when they decorated their cottages with greenery, exchanged presents, and ate and drank lustily in the festival they called 'Yule'. And when the Spring came, they, like the Romans, held another festival. The Romans' May festivities were dedicated to the goddess Flora, the Saxons to their own fertility goddess, but both festivals called for flowers and garlands, and much dancing and merry-making.

Rituals like these, rooted as they were in the fundamental hopes and needs of every human society, probably existed in this country long before the Romans or the Saxons came. The Roman occupation, indeed, was only to have a limited effect on our native patterns of behaviour. Most of the remnants of Roman festivals come to us at second hand, having filtered through to us from France, where Roman culture had a more permanent influence. The Saxons on the other hand came here to stay, and the old Celtic rituals were soon overlaid by the rites of their deeply feared gods and the festivals held in their honour.

The Coming of Christianity
When the first Christian missionaries came to England from Rome in the seventh century, they were deeply shocked by the pagan feast days and superstitions that even their most eager Christian converts seemed to cling to. Pope Gregory, to whom they appealed for advice, showed compassion and commonsense. He advised them not to try to wipe out the old beliefs completely, but to adapt them to coincide with Christian beliefs. In a letter to the perplexed Archbishop Mellitus in 601 AD, he advised: 'Where of old they were wont to sacrifice cattle to demons, thither let them continue to resort on the day of the saint to whom the church is dedicated, and slay their beasts no longer as a sacrifice, but for a social meal in honour of whom they now worship.'

So the Saxons were wisely allowed the comfort of their old festivals, now intermingled with their new religion. The Saxon Yule became incorporated in

2 Harvest was a busy time for the peasant, but he could enjoy the prospect of a merry time at the end of it.

the Christian Christmas. At the old Midwinter festival the little stone churches were wreathed in the traditional boughs of holly and yew (mistletoe was considered too powerful a pagan symbol to be really respectable) and presents were officially given in memory of the Wise Men's gifts, rather than in honour of a heathen goddess. The Spring festival still kept its old name of Eostre, but it now came to commemorate not the rebirth of the year but the resurrection of the Christian God. Harvest offerings were welcomed into the church, and their Christian relevance underlined by the priest reminding his people of the parable of the sower. The old pagan fertility charm – the corn spirit, or 'corn dolly', was also benignly accepted by the priest and fastened to the chancel screen. So, gently and irrevocably the old pagan observances were drawn into the Christian year. Old rituals took on a new meaning – and as men rested or danced and feasted on their holy days, they gradually forgot the old gods to whom they had once been dedicated.

The Mediaeval Holy Day
It is, perhaps, impossible for us, living in modern times, to understand the power of the mediaeval church and its total dominion over the hearts and minds of its people. The whole existence of mediaeval man, woman, or child lay under its influence; they were comforted by its sacraments, protected by its charity, and disciplined by its threats of eternal damnation. The old rites and superstitions of pagan times which it had so shrewdly and adroitly absorbed, served only to strengthen its place in its people's hearts, and to guarantee their unquestioning acceptance of its doctrine and authority.

Just as the Church's teaching was at the heart of mediaeval man's view of the world, so was the church building and its priest at the centre of his everyday life. Not only was he baptised and married there, and buried within its grounds, but he also used it as a meeting place and refuge, and his leisure time was centred on its festivals. Mediaeval holy days were very much holidays, and enjoyable ones too – though in an age with little transport, they were inevitably holidays at home.

There were certainly plenty of them. The official celebration of Christmas took fourteen days, and there were in addition the great festivals of Easter and Whitsuntide, as well as the many saint's days. These were obligatory holidays on which all work was supposed to stop. There were also, of course, fifty-two Sundays for which the mediaeval peasant had good reason to be thankful.

Not all lords of the manor were generous enough to grant all the holidays that their peasants were entitled to – even some of the abbots and bishops who controlled manors on behalf of the Church were parsimonious about this matter. For all men, even the holiest, lived by the land, and therefore tolerated, 'Erynge, sowynge, repynge, mowyng and cartyng' on holy days, as long as it was done out of 'necessitye' rather than 'avaryce'. Some manors got away with allowing their peasants only one holy day off in two, so anxious were they not to give up too much of the 'boon work' that the villagers owed to their lord, and on which the manors depended. The peasant himself made no complaint against the occasional non-observance of holy days and was grateful when his priest allowed him to spend some of his Sunday, after Mass, on his own strips of land. For landless labourers, especially, holy days could mean a considerable loss of income, for they were dependent on a daily wage, and no work meant no pay. They must often have tried to get round the problem by working surreptitiously, for in 1403 a law was passed forbidding labourers to offer their services for hire on the Lord's day. In the main, however, the mediaeval peasant welcomed the holy days with delight and relief, for they brought a break in a life of hard work, scant reward and monotonous diet.

At Christmas, above all, he could be sure of a good time. There was a considerable element of the old Roman topsy-turvydom during this festival. Boy bishops were appointed to preach sermons and 'Lords of Misrule' were given the job of supervising scenes of wild buffoonery. Perhaps even more wonderful to the peasant were the great feasts that his lord provided, sometimes even waiting on the villagers himself. A good fire was built in the hall, each serf bringing logs to keep it burning. He would also bring with him his own dish and mug, and in some manors he was asked to bring his own napkin in case he disliked eating from a bare table. In the diocese of Wells in the fourteenth century, the peasants were expected 'to take away anything that was left, in his cloth and he shall have for his neighbours one wastel (loaf) cut in three'. There was always plenty of broth and bread for him to eat his fill, and more remarkable, two kinds of meat – a great luxury to men who ate meat rarely and only in small quantities.

All mediaeval feasts were colourful, but never can colour have been more appreciated than at this time of cold and darkness. For a brief time life was warm and bright with firelight and candles and the peasants' huts were cheered by the greenery that carried echoes of a pagan past. Central to it all was the Christmas story which played its own part in bringing pageantry, excitement and perhaps a little tenderness to soften a somewhat harsh world.

Each great day in the Church's calendar brought similar scenes of gaiety and more dramatic stories to be told. At Easter the story of the resurrection was acted out by unskilled players; hot cross buns were baked and a few crumbs carefully stored away to be used as a greatly valued cure for all kinds of ailments; eggs, the symbol of new life, were boiled hard and dyed in different colours. On Shrove Tuesday, the last normal day before the austerities of Lent, pancakes were eaten and an especially rowdy game of football played. Rogation tide, at the end of April, brought a striking blend of the pagan and Christian rituals. The traditional procession to ask the corn god to bless the crops still persisted, but it had now become part of the Church's own ritual, and the priest himself now led his people through the fields.

Religion old and new thus played a part in forming man's concept of a holiday, but there were secular influences too. However devout, however conscious of his

3 Mummers entertaining guests at a feast.

need for salvation, the mediaeval peasant knew that his survival on earth depended on the land and the crops that he could coax out of it. Some of his merriest festivals were still held at moments of special importance in the farming year. The end of hay cutting was an occasion when the lord expressed his thanks for a job well done by giving his peasants a meal and by turning a sheep loose into the field as a prize for whoever could catch it. On May Day, when the fruit blossom was flowering and the corn was shooting up, the whole village would go out early into the fields to bring back flowers and branches of blossoming hawthorn, though great care was taken that none of it should come too near their houses lest ill luck might follow. Later in the year when the harvest was safely in there would be another feast in the manor yard, with trestle tables bearing cauldrons of steaming pottage, plenty of ale, and 'cheese at call'.

Mediaeval 'Ales'

'Ales' were another opportunity for a holiday and a break in routine. These were mediaeval versions of our bazaars or fetes, and were organized by the lord or his bailiff as fund-raising affairs which all peasants were compelled to attend and to buy a specified quantity of ale. At Glastonbury, the tenants were summoned to attend ales three times a year. At Michaelmas they were obliged to spend threepence; after Michaelmas there were two more restrained occasions where they were only required to spend two and a half pence.

The peasants themselves organised 'bride ales' for newly married couples. After the church ceremony the whole party would return to the village ale house and there they would buy their own home brewed ale, all proceeds going to set up the young couple in their new home.

The priests found these 'ales' a continual source of spiritual danger to their flock, for the drinking and merry-making often got out of hand. Bishop Poore of Salisbury had obviously been shocked by such goings-on when he ordered in 1223 'that marriages should be celebrated reverently and with honour, not with laughter or sport, or in taverns or at public potations or feasts'. The custom, however, was much too enjoyable to be stamped out even by such invective, and a good ration of ale continued to be a highly prized part of a wedding feast. In the end the Church itself found that the custom of 'ales' could be turned to good account, as groups of parishioners organized 'churchyard ales' to pay for repairs to the church buildings.

Holiday Games

Most holy days were an excuse for games and sport of all kinds both in town and country. We have a vivid and detailed account of some of these in the work of William Fitzstephen, a twelfth-century historian who recorded the pleasures of holy days in London. 'Every year', he wrote, 'at Shrove Tuesday, the school boys do bring Cockes of the game to their Master, and all the forenoon delight themselves in Cockfighting; after dinner all the youthes go into the field to play at bal . . . the aunciet and wealthy men of the Citie come forth on horse back to see the sport of the young men, and to take part of the pleasure of beholding their agilitie. . . . In the Holye days they fight battailes on the water. . . . In the Holye days all the Somer the youths are exercised in leaping, dancing, shooting, wrestling, casting their stone, and practising their shields; the maidens trip their timbrels, and daunce as long as they can well see. In Winter, every holy day before dinner, the Boares prepared for brawne are set to fight, or else Buls and Beares are baited.'

The 'bal' that the youths played at was probably football, though a football somewhat different from the modern version and ungraced by any rules. It was played sometimes by hundreds of people at a time over large areas of land, and seems to have been the excuse for a glorious if somewhat bloody rough and tumble,

4 Jousting provided a favourite mediaeval spectacle.

often leading to serious brawls, and it was regarded by many priests as a snare of the devil!

The dancing that accompanied such occasions also gave rise to some angry sermons, for it too often tempted men away from church on holy days, and moreover led to 'unclene kyssinge and other unhonest handelynges'. The priests might chide but the dance went on. The same pagan element in the dancing that disturbed so many priests in fact ensured its survival; its roots lay too deep to be dislodged even by threats of hell fire. Morris dances, for instance, which are still performed in some English villages today, are thought to be a relic of the old fertility rites, with leaping intended to persuade the crops to spring from the earth, and bells to frighten away evil spirits.

Holiday plays

Most of the important holy days were made specially exciting by the visits of the mummers, and by the performance of Miracle plays. Mumming was a simple form of acting which went back to the far off times when the gods had to be propitiated by the sacrifice of a victim. As the centuries passed, a live victim was no longer considered necessary. It was thought enough to act out the killing in a dance, though still impressing the gods with the vigour of the preliminary sword play. By the Middle Ages these dances had developed into simple plays, with a hero who always died, but who was always miraculously restored to life by a learned doctor – a character who most probably had originated in the tribal medicine man. The mummers who presented these plays were usually local people who travelled round the villages on holy days, enlivening their simple but immensely popular stories with slapstick comedy and acrobatics.

The Miracle or Mystery Plays were entirely Christian. They were simple plays originally organized by the clergy, usually in the nave or chancel of the church, to

5 Hunting was the favourite leisure activity of the mediaeval nobleman.

explain to their uneducated congregations certain key events or mysteries in the church's calendar. Over the years the plays became much more elaborate and their performance was sometimes taken over by the craft gilds, which often selected stories with a particular relevance to their own trade. At first the plays were performed on scaffolding erected for the occasion in the market place. Eager spectators crowded round, and householders hung out of their windows to see the fun. Later a series of pageant wagons were used, each one depicting a different scene or 'mansion' of the narrative. Gradually, instead of making up the words as they went along, they wrote down the dialogue – the first play scripts ever to be used. Some, whose words were particularly moving and entertaining, like those of York, are still performed today. The religious teaching that the plays contained may seem primitive and crude to modern minds, with angels climbing up to heaven on real ladders, jaws of hell that really opened and shut, and black, blue and red devils jumping out to sieze the poor damned souls – but to mediaeval man it was unbeatable entertainment, bringing thrills and drama to his holy day.

6 Holy days were still high days of merry-making in Tudor times.

7 The Victorians revived the old pagan custom of decorating the house with trees and boughs of evergreens.

Fairs

The plays, whether acted by mummers or gildsmen, were local entertainments. The peasant could enjoy them in his own village, the trader or merchant in his own town. This was just as well at a time when the only form of transport for most people was a pair of poorly shod feet. But sometimes there came the chance of a really superb occasion – the Fair – and for that it was worth trudging many miles. The mediaeval fairs were held at the great festivals, and only in certain towns. Protected by royal charter, they were essential centres of mediaeval trade and commerce, not just for England but for the whole of Europe. They gave to the peasant a rare glimpse of visitors from strange lands, with their odd speech and exotic wares – furs, silks, scents, and spices. They could enjoy looking at the work of the local goldsmiths, the toy makers, milliners and drapers, and though they could never afford to buy any of their goods, which were designed for the noble and the wealthy, they might at least be able to take home something small – a 'fairing' – like a bunch of ribbons or a simple wooden toy or just a piece of gingerbread. Most exciting of all were the sideshows – acrobats, mummers, wild beasts, dwarves and jugglers – the memory of them a gift of colour and comedy to last him through many a year.

So holy days during the Middle Ages saw the development of pleasures which were increasingly centred on man's enjoyment, rather than on the worship of God. Men and women began to look forward to holy days not only because of their religious significance, though this was still immensely important, but because they were happy times when work was forgotten, and when they could escape through play and pageantry into a world of greater colour and variety.

2 To Go on Pilgrimages

Mediaeval man tended to live out his life in one class of society and in one place. Wherever he lived – in cottage, workshop, monastery or palace – he expected to stay, doing the same job and in the same surroundings until he died. Moreover, the community he lived in was largely isolated from any other; it had to be self-sufficient because travel was difficult, and often dangerous. But the history of the Middle Ages is also the history of the partial breaking down of this enforced separateness. As trade increased between different areas and with other countries, more and more people had to take to the roads, and the traffic of pedlars, packmen, court officials, and great lords moving from one manor to another, gradually increased. Among these travellers were the pilgrims, journeying perhaps to Canterbury or Walsingham, or to the channel ports, on the way to Compostela or Jerusalem for the good of their souls. And in their written accounts of these journeys they showed a delight in novelty, in adventure and travel for its own sake, that was in later years to become such an important part of an English holiday.

8 The stones of Avebury – the destination of pre-Christian pilgrims.

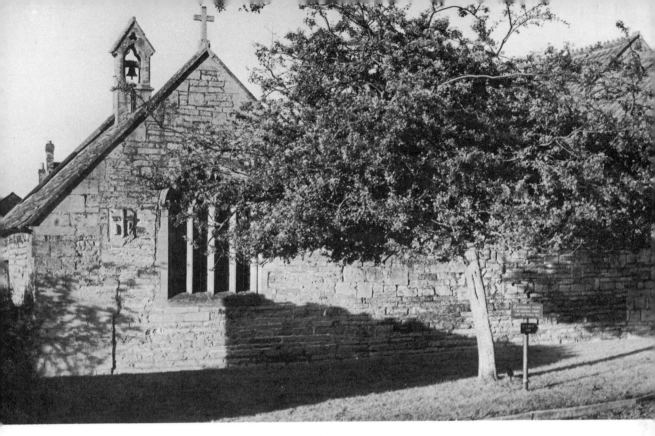

9 Many pilgrims in the Middle Ages journeyed to Glastonbury to see the miraculous thorn tree, which they believed grew on the spot where St. Joseph of Arimsthaea had stuck his staff into English soil.

The Origins of Pilgrimages

The idea of journeying to places with sacred associations is older than Christianity. Anyone who has seen the avenue of stones leading across the fields to the great Celtic monument at Avebury has seen a pilgrim road once used by travellers from the Continent as well as from Britain, as they came to this place where they felt especially close to their gods. In the same way the early Christians longed to feel near to Jesus and his disciples. Sometimes they chose to go to the Holy Land to see for themselves the places where they had lived and taught; sometimes they set out to visit Rome, where the Christian Church had first become a reality; sometimes they visited the shrines of the saints and martyrs who had died or suffered for its sake.

Eusebius of Caesarea tells us in his writings that as early as the beginning of the third century, bishops from Cappadocia made the pilgrimage to Rome. Helena, the mother of Constantine, in 362 AD travelled to Jerusalem where her son ordered a Christian church to be built over the sepulchre where Jesus had lain after his crucifixion. Over the years the flow of pilgrims increased despite the interruptions of the wars that troubled Europe and which periodically swept through the Middle East.

The mediaeval pilgrim, of course, was hoping not only to feel inspired by his visits to the Holy Land or to the shrines of the saints; in many cases he was seeking a cure for illness; he certainly believed he was ensuring the salvation of his soul. This idea that pilgrimages would ensure escape from the torments of hell and shorten the inevitable stay in purgatory became widely accepted in the Middle Ages though a few of the clergy had their doubts. Saint Boniface in the eighth century was pretty sure that however pure the motives of female pilgrims, they were almost certain to lose their virtue on the way! Saint Thomas à Kempis felt that 'those who wander much are but little hallowed', and the fifteenth-century English Dominican John Bromyard felt that many pilgrims made their pilgrimage away from God into the arms of the devil, rather than the other way round. Certainly it was an idea later to be bitterly attacked by the Lollards and by the theologians of the Reformation.

Nevertheless, however powerful and eloquent the attacks, pilgrimages continued throughout the Middle Ages, and gradually a whole body of customs and rules, something, indeed, approaching a system of organisation grew up around them.

Preparations

In many ways the pilgrim was a privileged person, He was often given special protection and services, helped on his way by gifts of money, and listened to on his return with the deference due to a holy man. For this reason special care was taken to see that his journey was in fact a genuine pilgrimage, and not just a means of acquiring prestige. Before he set out on his journey he was supposed to have written permission from a bishop, or from his abbot if he were a monk, and he was advised to see that his family was provided for, that his business affairs were in order and that his will was made. This was particularly important, of course, if he was journeying abroad. He also had to equip himself with money for his journey, often by arranging drafts on foreign merchants at Winchester fair, which was held once a year and was a common centre for pilgrims' currency arrangements.

If we are to believe the evidence of Chaucer's *Canterbury Tales*, pilgrims going to shrines in this country did not always wear special clothing. Chaucer's pilgrims – and how like modern holiday makers they were – wore all sorts of fashions, including the much embroidered outfit of the gay young squire. Generally, however, the 'roamers' bound for Rome, and the 'palmers' off to the Holy Land or other 'straunge strandes', wore garments specially designed for their journey.

On this point we are indebted, as for so much other information, to a fifteenth-century Dominican friar from Zurich, Brother Felix Fabri, who left three large volumes of detailed reminiscences, in which, he says, he had 'dared among great things and true, to mingle things silly, improbable and comical'. He tells us that there were 'five outward badges of a pilgrim, to wit – a red cross on a long grey

10 Pilgrims drawn from many ranks of mediaeval society leave Canterbury.

gown, with the monk's cowl sewn to the tunic. . . . The second is a black or grey hat, marked in front with a red cross. . . . The third is a long beard growing from a face that is pale and serious. . . . The fourth is the scrip on his shoulders, containing his slender provisions, with a bottle – sufficient not for luxury but barely for the necessaries of life. The fifth, which he assumes only in the Holy Land is an ass, with a Saracen driver, instead of his staff.' If he were journeying to an English shrine like Glastonbury, Walsingham or Canterbury, his preparations would be a much simpler matter, particularly if he were lucky enough to find a genial organizer like Chaucer's landlord. Then if weather and company were pleasant, he could really feel in holiday mood as he 'cantered' to Canterbury along the Pilgrim's Way through the pleasant countryside.

A journey abroad demanded both more elaborate preparations and greater courage. One of the most popular places of pilgrimage for the English was Compostela in Spain, where the body of St James – Sant' Iago – was believed to have been buried. To get there the pilgrim had to take ship for the ports of Normandy or Bordeaux, and then make his way on foot or on hired horses along the recognised pilgrims' routes through France. All these roads met at Saint-Jean-Pied-de-Port in the Pyrenees where the traveller crossed via Cise and Roncevaux into Spain. It was a long and wearisome journey but for people who had seen little of the world beyond their own district, it must have been one of beguiling novelty. There were inns and hospices along the route, and the pilgrims were not entirely without guidance – certain roads and inns would be widely known, and their faults or virtues must have been a topic of conversation along the way. Moreover, for those who could read there were the mediaeval equivalents of our present day guide books – volumes of chatty and useful anecdotes like those of Aimery Picaud, a twelfth-century monk from Poitou who wrote a most excellent *Guide du Pelerin* (Pilgrim's Guide). His accounts of food and local customs of the

French provinces through which the pilgrim would pass are perhaps over-critical, except when he is talking about his native Poitou, but he gives some useful hints. Many pilgrims must have had cause to be grateful for his advice on how to protect themselves from the horse-flies of the Landes region, or for his warnings about the Gascons, who, he claimed, 'eat a lot, drink at a gulp and are badly dressed' or his instructions how best to board the small ferry boat which crossed a river near Santiago itself. They may indeed have been a little alarmed by his bitter accounts of the toll officials of the Basque country, 'who come out in front of pilgrims with two or three staves to exact an unjust tax by force . . . cursing him and searching him down to his breeches'. Nevertheless, besides being practically useful, the Guide must have given a spice of adventure and curiosity to many a traveller, even before he set off.

The pilgrims to Compostela, to Rome and to the Holy Land must, of course, have been enormously reassured to learn of the network of assistance provided by the orders of knighthood specially formed to protect the Holy Places and to help the pilgrims on their way. The Knights of Malta for instance was an order which had originally been founded in Jerusalem to run a rest house and infirmary for pilgrims; their order only became a military one after the Moslem attacks on Christians, after which the pilgrims needed them as defenders as well as hosts. The Knights Templar were a similar order; they, too, offered a network of help and protection for pilgrims, and indeed, as a consequence of their skill in currency arrangements came to be used as bankers throughout Europe. The monasteries also played their part in succouring the travellers, as they moved along the routes of Europe. Their best plate and most lavish fare were naturally reserved for those who could pay for them, but to all pilgrims they gave aid and shelter as they needed them.

The inns, like present day hotels, were unpredictable; some were clean and pleasant, providing good food and wine – others were less obliging, and infested not only with fleas but with robbers. Where there were no inns or monasteries alternative accommodation had to be found. Fabri records that in Corfu some of the pilgrims clubbed together to hire a house; and in Crete an obliging brothel keeper bustled his courtesans out of his house and scrubbed it thoroughly so that the pilgrims should have somewhere to stay!

Staying in Venice
However many the pilgrims' vicissitudes on their way across Europe, on arrival at Venice they must have felt that at last they were in a place fully geared to their needs, whose citizens could offer them an expertise born of long experience in arranging transport to the Holy Land. It was a city whose wealth and importance had been built on its geographical position – a city that linked the world of Europe with the trade routes of the East; and therefore the point where many of the pilgrims' routes converged for the passage by sea to the Holy Land. The state of

11 These mediaeval pilgrims seem to have taken their journey very seriously.

Venice, naturally, had a commercial interest in pilgrimages but fortunately for the pilgrims, its officials showed a marked sense of responsibility for their welfare, and applied to their problems a thoroughness which would do credit to a twentieth-century travel agency.

The inns were licensed by the state and therefore had to conform to certain standards. 'Piazza guides' were appointed; two of them were supposed to be at their posts on the Rialto or in the Piazza of Saint Mark from dawn to dusk. Their job was to provide an information bureau for the pilgrims, advising them on currency, helping them with their language difficulties, directing them to the most reputable tradesmen and arranging contact for them with the captains of the pilgrims galleys. Certainly the pilgrims needed help, for they had a lot of shopping to do before they set off, if they were to equip themselves properly for their voyage. Fabri tells of expeditions to the market to buy 'cushions, mattresses, pillows, sheets, coverlets, mats, jars, and so forth'. The guides would advise them to buy their bedding from a man near St Mark's; to get their water for the journey from the well of Saint Nicholas; to buy the wine of Padua for storing on the journey. Many pilgrims were sceptical of the galley captains' promises to supply two meals a day, and thoughtfully provided themselves with hams, ox-tongues, salt bacon, cheese, bread and biscuits. The most fastidious also took care to take spices with which to make unsavoury food more palatable, and added dried apples, figs, and raisins to their store. One Italian writer adds for good measure, a hint that it might be advisable to 'hire a cage for half a dozen hens or chickens ... And buy you half a bushel of millet seed at Venice for them'.

The next and even more crucial task was to find a ship. Here again the city of Venice provided an excellent service, although it was often hard put to it to protect the pilgrims from the profiteering of the ships' captains. The most stringent rules were laid down to ensure the safety of the ships. Each galley was to have a cross painted on the hull, and was not to be loaded beyond this point; captains were to be over thirty, and sailors were made to swear an oath that they would look after the ship and its cargo. Every attempt was made to see that the contracts between captain and passenger were properly drawn up and duly honoured. The fare, ranging from 30 to 60 ducats, was supposed to cover not only the cost of the return journey to Jaffa, but also two hot meals with good wine and the expenses of arranging transport and safe conducts on arrival.

The Voyage
The voyage was an adventure, certainly, but one that was often too exciting and dangerous to be pleasurable. The calls at foreign ports and the difficulty of preserving food, made threat of disease constant, and in the crowded and often insanitary conditions of the pilgrim galleys, disease could spread rapidly. The ships, however strictly inspected by the authorities, were not always proof against the storms that could suddenly blow up and many pilgrims had the equally frightening experience, as Fabri did, of seeing the ship becalmed, or kept out of harbour by contrary winds, knowing that their precious stocks of water and food were fast running out, and watching their thirsty livestock pathetically licking the dew from the decks. Perhaps most daunting of all was the fear of attack from pirates or Turks.

Nevertheless there were compensations. There was plenty of advice available as to how to make the voyage as comfortable as possible. William Wey, an English priest of the fifteenth century, firmly advised, 'Be sure if you go in a galley to choose a place on the upper stage, for in the lowest it is right smouldering hot and stinking'. Fabri even took the trouble to issue a warning that a pilgrim should 'be careful where he sits down . . . for every place is covered with pitch which becomes soft in the heat of the sun.' They could also learn from seasoned travellers the wrinkle of storing their wine and eggs in the sand ballast under the planks of their cabins to keep them cool.

Life on the galleys was something of a scramble, with pilgrims rushing at the sound of the trumpet to get a reasonable place at meal times. The wine was often watered and their possessions were often stolen by the galley slaves who then sold them for a handsome sum at the next port. Yet despite these snags there was time to talk, and as Fabri said, 'On board ship many pleasant and jolly friendships are made'. The pilgrims according to him found plenty of ways to pass the time – gambling, singing, running up the rigging, weight lifting, drinking, or passing the whole time asleep in their berths or sometimes just sitting and looking at the sea.

12 (*Opposite*) Pilgrims enjoyed collecting these badges to show the places they had visited, and they conferred great prestige on the wearer.

The Arrival

On arrival at Jaffa it was the captain's job to bargain for the hire of asses on which to continue the journey, and to arrange safe conducts. There was often a delay, during which the poor pilgrims were consigned sometimes for days on end, to a row of filthy caves on the sea shore. Sometimes there was trouble with the captains themselves. Once the arrangements were made they thought only of the return journey and made the long-suffering pilgrims rush their tour of the Holy Places in a much shorter time than originally agreed, and all too often they returned from Jerusalem exhausted and dissatisfied.

Whatever the dangers of the journey, whatever the problems on landing, the first sight of Jerusalem, the Holy City, was a moment of great joy and thankfulness. The pilgrims would kneel on the dusty road and offer up prayers of gratitude. As they entered Jerusalem, they would first make their way to the Church of the Holy Sepulchre where many of them indulged in tears and wailing – Fabri rather acidly observed that this 'was not because of the power the place exercises over them . . . but because of the ease with which they weep.'

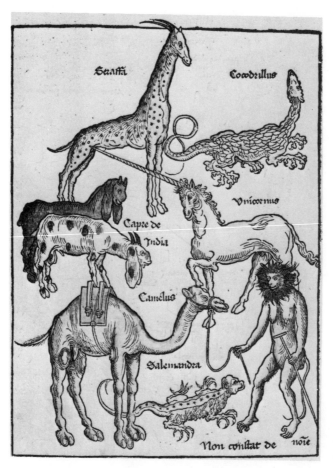

13 The animals that von Breydenbach claimed to have seen in the Holy Land.

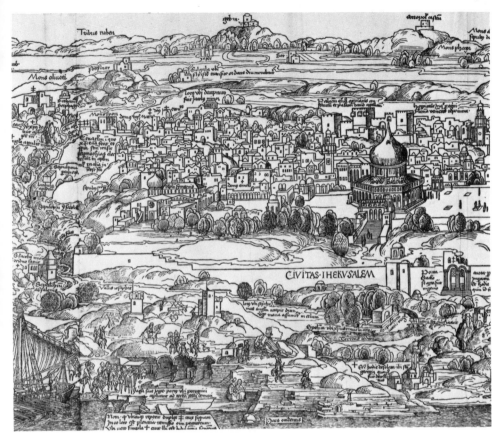

14 Jerusalem as Bernard von Breydenbach's artist depicted it.

There were various places to stay in Jerusalem. The galley captains usually stayed at the Franciscan house on Mount Zion, though the Franciscans themselves were suspicious of such worldly company and preferred to entertain only members of religious orders. There was also the hospital of Saint John, which was contemptuously described by one pilgrim as 'a very poor place' though we know that pilgrims who stayed there were at least provided with carpets to sleep on.

The stay in Jerusalem was as strenuous as the most efficiently organized sightseeing tour today. The pilgrim was conducted round every place that had even the remotest connection with the New Testament – even to what was supposed to be the very pillar on which the cock crew after Peter's denials of Christ. There were also 'half day excursions' to the valleys and hills nearby, and longer tours to Bethlehem, Jordan and the Dead Sea.

The last days of the visit were spent not only in a final vigil at the Holy Sepulchre and in second visits to places of special importance, but also in determined souvenir hunting. Many of these small treasures surprisingly foreshadow the souvenirs of a much later age – wooden models of the chapel of Calvary, or of the

Church at Bethlehem, 'or a crucifix in a paper enclosed with boards'. Some of the pilgrims were so anxious to keep a part of this wonderful place with them for the rest of their lives, that they chipped off fragments of the buildings to take home with them, believing that these precious relics would afford them protection against dangers and disease. The richer pilgrims could afford to buy splendid things with which to impress their families – lengths of damask cloth, deerskin gloves, cloth of gold, and chests made of cypress wood. Much more truly devout and for us four hundred years later perhaps more touching was Fabri's choice of memento. He simply collected from Mount Zion and from the Mount of Olives a little bag of pebbles, and laboriously gathered under a scorching sun some of the thorns that grew on the hedgerows.

The End of Pilgrimages
With the approach of the sixteenth century and the gradual spread of the ideas of the Reformation, pilgrimages, like indulgences and relics came under sustained and powerful attack. The simple credulity and uneducated piety could not withstand that growing sense of curiosity and scepticism which characterised the European Renaissance. With the coming of the Modern Age pilgrims ceased to make their way along the roads of Europe.

Yet even now in the middle of the twentieth century we still make our own kind of pilgrimages. We still make long and sometimes expensive journeys to those cities which have a special place in our hearts. We travel not in search of remedies or an easy entry into heaven, but because we want to come as close as we can to the lives of saints, or writers or composers whom we particularly revere.

We still share with those early pilgrims the delight in new and exciting experiences, that so many of them found on the way. As we click our cameras we might remember Bernhard von Breydenbach, a pilgrim who lived at the same time as Brother Fabri. He could not take a camera; instead he took an artist with him to record all the things on his journey that were as he put it, 'fair and lovely to the eye'.

3 Waddling to the Waters

During the Middle Ages, many sick and crippled pilgrims had embarked on their journeys not only in search of salvation for their souls, but in the hope of a cure for their sick bodies. This belief in supernatural remedies still acts today as a powerful motive for many incurably sick people, sending them in thousands every year to shrines like that at Lourdes.

The Origin of the Spa
On the whole, however, the widespread faith in miraculous cures began to disappear from Europe with the end of the Middle Ages. The theologians of the Reformation denounced such ideas as superstitions, and the Renaissance, with its emphasis on knowledge and scientific study, encouraged men to seek for less mystical remedies. Undoubtedly one of the most favoured of these new cures was drinking, or bathing in mineral waters.

15 Rowlandson's cartoon shows a motley gathering of patients queueing up for their glass of mineral water.

It was not an entirely new idea. People have always regarded natural springs with a certain awe, particularly when they are hot or heavily mineralised. The waters of Bath were quite probably used as a medicine even before the Romans came, and we know what enthusiasm they were to bring to the taking of the waters. With the Renaissance, the mineral springs throughout Europe assumed even more importance, and just as many of the saints had their shrines so many of the springs were to become the location of new towns – the spas, given over to the pursuit of health. It was a fashion that was to create new wealth, new pastimes, and provide a splendid new excuse for staying away from home for long periods of delightful leisure – for taking a holiday.

During the Tudor and Stuart periods England gradually acquired the cult of the Spa, and even the Civil War did nothing to dislodge the new fashion. Bath's relatively palatable waters were prescribed by doctors all over England for a variety of ailments and above all, as an excellent remedy for ladies who were unable to conceive children (or as some doctors delicately put it, 'ladies that gave a desire to be gott with child'). This reputation was enhanced after the visit of Catherine of Braganza, the queen of Charles II. She, poor lady, longed for a child, and did in fact become pregnant after her stay in Bath. Although her hopes were dashed when the baby miscarried, the waters' potency as a wonder fertility drug was felt by many credulous people to have been triumphantly vindicated.

Not everyone could manage the journey to Bath. Fortunately there were other places whose waters became equally prized. Tunbridge Wells, a town which owes its existence entirely to its reputation as a watering place, became a favourite

16 Taking the waters at Tunbridge Wells in the seventeenth century.

resort of the fashionable London circles. The waters there were found to be chalybeate – rich in iron – and were considered excellent for the prevention of consumption. Queen Henrietta Maria was certainly convinced of their value; in 1629 she stayed there for six weeks probably using a tent for her accommodation, as did so many other visitors to this as yet undeveloped spa.

Northern gentlemen and their families were delighted when a local doctor, Robert Wittie assured them that the Scarborough waters would cure 'the Apoplexie, Epilepsie, Catalepsie, Vertigo, the Jaunders both black and yellow' and were in addition, 'almost Soveraign remedy against Hypochondriach Melancholy and Windiness.' Visitors to Scarborough got a special bonus in that they also discovered the delights of sea-side air. Those of them who went on to sample the newly re-discovered waters of Harrogate also no doubt found the air invigorating and some compensation for having to swallow the 'stinking waters' whose efficacy was thought to lie in their sulphur content.

Unpleasant conditions in Eighteenth-century Spas

The unpleasant taste of the waters was not the only thing about the new spas to offend their visitors. Although they appreciated the growing efforts of the various corporations and entrepreneurs to provide them with pleasant accommodation and entertainment, they found that the pursuit of health had its sordid side. Fashionable visitors taking treatment for slight, even imaginary ailments found that they had to rub shoulders with genuinely sick, sometimes dying patients who were not at all fashionable, but poor, disfigured and dirty. Certainly the corporation of Bath had made some effort to stop the really serious pollution of the waters by forbidding in 1646 the throwing of rubbish, including dead dogs. Nevertheless, bathing there, even in the second half of the eighteenth century, could be disconcerting, and though the scientific explanation of infectious disease was as yet unknown, many people guessed that a dip in such squalid waters might provide them with a new disease rather than with a cure! Pepys, when describing in his diary a visit to Bath in 1688, typically commented that: 'Much company come; very fine ladies; and the manner pretty enough . . . only methinks it can not be clean to go so many bodies together in the same water.'

Smollet, in *Humphrey Clinker*, a novel published over half a century later, is even more trenchant in his criticism. 'Good Heavens, the very thought makes my blood run cold. We know not what sores may be running into the water while we are bathing, and what sort of matter we may thus imbibe; the king's evil, the scurvy, the cancer, and the pox.' His Mr Bramble is, if anything, even more appalled when he suspects that due to faulty drainage, the water the visitors are given to drink was quite likely no more than the filtered water from the dirty baths.

Visitors to most of the watering places found that uncongenial company was not restricted to the baths themselves. The streets were often dirty and full of beggars, and in Bath particularly, the local servants had a reputation for surliness

17 Patients bathing in the King's and Queen's bath.

and a resentful attitude to the unwelcome visitors. The men who carried the sedan chairs were notorious for their habit of refusing to let a passenger leave a chair, unless he paid the often extortionate fare demanded of him. Inns were generally well below the standard of comfort expected by fashionable society, and lodgings were scarce and expensive. What buildings had been provided were surrounded by slums and shanties, and if we are to believe the stringent criticisms of the Duchess of Marlborough, there was 'never any place abroad that had more stinks in it and dirt than Bath.' It hardly seems possible that the journey, over poor roads and the footpad infested Claverton Down, could have been worth the effort.

The Advent of Beau Nash

Fortunately, even during the time that Smollett was making Mr Bramble complain so bitterly, an energetic, resourceful and redoubtable gentleman – Richard Nash – was already about his work of tidying up and organizing not only Bath, but indirectly, the whole of English fashionable society. He was giving the pastime of a holiday at a fashionable health resort a new flavour – of elegance, order and refinement.

He was, when one comes to think of it, an unlikely candidate for the job. Indeed it is hardly likely that the corporation of Bath would ever have considered him as their Master of Ceremonies if they had examined the less praiseworthy aspects of his undistinguished career. He had committed, for example the grave error of being humbly born. His father was an insignificant Welsh business man. Richard had been up at Oxford which might have brightened the picture, except that he was sent down after only four terms leaving his debts behind him. His career as an ensign was hardly more glorious; he liked the uniform but found the life distasteful. He then tried the law, but used it only as a stepping stone to amusing and fashionable society. Nevertheless he had certain qualities which recommended him to the worthy city fathers of Bath. He had had the luck in 1695 to direct a pageant organized by his fellow students for the entertainment of King William III, and it was a great success. Nash was in fact offered a knighthood on the strength of it but could not afford to accept it. The reputation which this success gave him was to serve him remarkably well, and it was reinforced by his other talents – wit, brilliant organizing ability, and most important of all, overpowering self assurance.

The Regime of Beau Nash

Once he took it in hand, Bath was never quite the same again. He had already served his apprenticeship, as social assistant to Captain Webster, Bath's first Master of Ceremonies, and when Nash took over the job in 1705 after Webster's death in a duel he knew exactly what was needed. He got rid of the beggars and

18 Beau Nash, who brought order and discipline to fashionable life in Bath.

the pitiful, shaven-headed lunatics who were wont to roam the streets, and disciplined the unruly servants and sedan chair carriers. Nor did the upper classes escape his attentions; he established rules of civilised conduct which were to ricochet through the drawing rooms of England. He forbade the wearing of swords, thus preventing the fights that were liable to break out so easily wherever gentlemen got together and drink flowed freely. He deplored the boorish habits of the country gentry and firmly forbade the wearing of boots at any of the gatherings he so carefully organized. Any gentleman so misguided as to wear them or to smoke a clay pipe was firmly shown the door. Aprons, for ladies, however pretty the apron or its wearer, were similarly deemed too reminiscent of the country and of serving wenches to be tolerated in polite society, and even the Duchess of Queensberry, who so far forgot herself as to enter the ballroom in an exquisite and expensive lace pinafore, had it peremptorily removed by an irate Master of Ceremonies. It is a measure of Nash's personality that she accepted the reproof with good humour.

He was equally firm in his disapproval of social snobbery. If a visitor to Bath knew how to conduct himself with propriety and in strict accordance with the Beau's rules, then he was welcome, however humble his birth. Any lady, however aristocratic, who was seen by him to decline an invitation to dance from a social inferior was liable to one of the Beau's crushing snubs. The one relic of the old

19 This picture of the Cross Bath shows the elegant architecture of eighteenth-century Bath.

20 Morning gossip became an essential part of the days' routine.

rumbustious way of life was gambling; this he loved too well to forbid, and indeed it was the basis of his fortune. Even so, he brought a new code of conduct into the gaming rooms. Players were expected to behave with dignity, to lose with good grace and to conduct their duels, which so often followed a gaming dispute, outside the city, and at an early hour, when they would cause the minimum disturbance.

Gradually, under his autocratic rule, visitors to Bath came to accept an unvarying and pleasant routine. Their arrival was usually heralded by a peal from the Abbey bells, and after such a rousing welcome no-one seems to have felt like complaining when they were later presented with the bill for the bell ringers' fees. Indeed they soon learned that the pleasures of Bath were all organized on a strict business basis.

From six to nine o'clock in the morning the visitors were expected to repair to the Baths for bodily refreshment. The ladies wore loose brown linen coats and petticoats, and chip bonnets; the gentlemen descended the green, slime-covered steps attired in jackets and drawers, topped by elegant three-cornered hats. In these garments they committed themselves to the water up to their necks, many of them shrieking from the shock. After all bathing was not in those days a common pastime, and the water in the King's bath was 103 degrees. No wonder the ladies carried handkerchiefs with which to wipe the sweat from their brows. However, in the Cross Bath, which was slightly cooler, there was more scope for enjoyment. The sexes were supposed to stay separate but this was difficult to enforce. As Daniel Defoe observed – 'the place being but narrow they converse freely, make vows, and sometimes love.' From time to time they would join cheerfully in the popular songs that the orchestra played for their entertainment. After all this they sank into sedan chairs and were taken back to their lodgings to change into elaborate dressing gowns, for a visit to the Pump Room where glasses of mineral water were served to them. This occasion was graced every morning, without fail, by the appearance of the Beau himself, dressed in the first style of elegance, and graciously chatting to a few favoured acquaintances. The gentlemen then visited the coffee house, the ladies one another's lodgings for rolls, Sally Lunns with plenty of butter and coffee. A visit to the Abbey for morning service was then obligatory for anyone aspiring to the first rank of fashion – and after that an hour or so was spent shopping, walking or browsing in the bookshops or circulating libraries, both of which thoughtfully provided chairs for loungers and gossipers as well as for readers. The more frivolous ladies had plenty of opportunity to spend money in the milliners' and dressmakers' shops in Milsom Street. The main meal of the day followed at 2 pm and however delicate they had felt their constitutions to be on arrival, they seem to have coped with rich and generous menus – 'boiled chicken, tongue, rabbits smothered in onions, roast beef, eggs in their shells, apple pie syllabub, claret, port' is a typical example. There was no opportunity to sleep it off, for after dinner everyone visited the Pump Room or

21 An evening ball in the Assembly Rooms.

took tea in the Assembly Rooms for the inexhaustible scandal and gossip that were the inevitable result of daily meetings in a restricted society. The evening was spent visiting the theatre, gambling or chatting, except for Tuesday and Friday nights when Balls were held in the Assembly Rooms starting at 6 pm sharp. Thousands of wax candles lit the beautifully proportioned rooms, crowded with fashionable visitors in their powdered wigs and beauty patches – the most resplendent of all being Beau Nash himself. He knew his business as a showman too well to be outshone, and his velvet and lace were always of the finest quality and richest colours, his wig the tallest in the room.

If much of this chapter has been devoted to Bath, rather than to the other eighteenth-century watering places, it is because Bath above all others became the envy and example of all the English spas. Nash had gauged the public taste with remarkable precision, and in many ways was to set the tone for the English resort for years to come. One can still find even today in many English seaside towns the same devotion to a gentle and untaxing routine, the same taste for morning coffee and gossip, the same kind of small and elegant shops that recall a more leisured age.

The Grand Tour

For some eighteenth-century gentlemen the visit to Bath or Buxton was but a tame affair. Many young men considered it the thing to travel abroad for a spell on the Continent. In this respect at least they were usually in agreement with their parents who considered the Grand Tour an indispensable part of a young nobleman's education. This idea of the leisurely extended tour abroad had developed from Tudor times, when young noblemen likely to be given jobs at court had been encouraged to travel in France and Italy, to improve their languages, to establish useful contacts and to acquire a polish glossier than that to be found in England.

Over a long period, fashionable life in England was looked down upon as lacking in refinement not only by European society but by many Englishmen themselves. They were quite ready humbly to agree with the Frenchman who commented rather superciliously 'They hum under their breath, they whistle, they sit down on a large arm chair and put their feet on another, they sit on any table in the room and do a thousand other things which would be quite ridiculous in France.' So while Beau Nash was doing his best to reform the manners of the country gentlemen in Bath, the more exalted and adventurous of their sons were sent to see if a little cosmopolitan elegance and refinement would rub off on to them.

Sometimes, if their parents could afford it, they were sent abroad for as long as five years. Usually they were accompanied by a tutor who was supposed not only to make them persevere with their studies, but also to see that they behaved themselves reasonably well. A really extensive tour might cost as much as five

22 A visit to Saint Peter's at Rome was considered essential for young men on the Grand Tour. They often tried to reproduce aspects of this kind of architecture in their own houses.

thousand pounds – in those days a small fortune. They usually spent some time in Paris visiting the French court, and joining in the life of any French families with whom their parents were acquainted. Here they would practise fencing, riding and billiards with French masters, before taking tours to Germany and Switzerland. The climax of the tour for those who had a genuine interest in the Arts came in Italy, where the grandeur of Roman architecture had been recently rediscovered, and where the achievements of the Renaissance must have dazzled eyes unprepared for their splendours.

The interiors of many English country houses still display the treasures that their eighteenth-century owners brought back from their European wanderings, and many of the exteriors show the taste they acquired for Italian architecture. Holkham Hall in Norfolk has an entrance hall designed in the form of a Roman basilica. The architects of Blenheim and Castle Howard and many other country houses tried, often with considerable success, to copy Italian building and decoration, not just because of their own preferences but because their patrons had, through travel, acquired the taste and knowledge to demand and to pay for that particular style. Sad to relate the Grand Tour was not always a cultural success story. Many a young man must have returned home spoiled by such a long period of undirected leisure, particularly if his poor tutor had given up the struggle to control him. No doubt some young noblemen in Adam Smith's dour words, returned home 'more conceited and unprincipled, more dissipated and more incapable of any serious application either to study or business than he could well have become in so short a time had he lived at home.'

Nevertheless, on balance the Grand Tour was to have a civilising and stimulating effect on English taste and manners. It awakened a new interest in foreign travel, and it left Europe with a string of hostelries geared to the strange demands of the English 'milor', and with a certain tolerance for his many oddities.

4 The Discovery of the Coast

The seas that surround Britain have protected her from attack, stimulated her trade and industry, and given her some of her most cherished heroes. Yet up to a hundred and fifty years ago few Britons ever saw the sea; for the roads were poor and few, and the coast for the most part was inaccessible, with little fishing villages tucked away at the foot of steep cliffs, or at the end of rough and muddy tracks. If the traveller did get a glimpse of the coast in the early days of the eighteenth century, he was unlikely to be impressed; in general he preferred his landscapes to be peaceful and ordered – wild waves and scudding clouds seemed to him altogether too savage and undisciplined for true beauty. The fisherman and the sailors knew the sea of course, respected it and even loved it – but as a source of their work and livelihood, and not of amusement or diversion. Only their children can have had the chance of occasionally enjoying those delightful inconsequential pleasures of the seaside that British children nowadays regard as an indispensable part of their holidays.

Some of those children who lived in remote fishing villages or in riverside hamlets must have learned to swim – Shakespeare talks of 'little wanton boys that swim on bladders'. They probably had more chance of a swim than their more privileged young countrymen, for even in the sixteenth century – not exactly a prudish age – there was a feeling among the upper classes that bathing (which was always nude bathing) was too reminiscent of Roman decadence to be tolerated. Young undergraduates at Cambridge in those days, who succumbed even in the hottest summers to the temptation of stripping off their clothes and plunging into the water, were punished by a double flogging!

However, during the late seventeenth century certain events and new ideas changed all this. Sea bathing not only became a respectable pastime even for the most elevated members of society but one that was warmly recommended by the highest medical authorities.

Mineral water cures by the Sea

Scarborough as we have already seen in the last chapter was the first of the fishing villages to be developed into a fashionable resort. This was not due to its attractive coastline but to a walk that a certain Mrs Farrow, a lady of gentle birth and 'delicate sensibilities', took along its foreshore in the year 1626. It was a walk that was to give the history of holidays an entirely new direction. Mrs Farrow noticed a russet coloured spring of water issuing out of one of the cliff rocks, and discovered that it had a metallic tang. This was a time, of course when the new

23 Sea dipping was considered an excellent cure even for George III's madness.

fashion of taking mineral waters was getting firmly into its stride, and Mrs Farrow's discovery meant that the ladies and gentlemen of Yorkshire now had a spa on their own doorstep.

Mrs Farrow's walk would not have been so portentous, without the publication of certain medical treatises some years later which drew the attention of the people of Scarborough and other seaside resort spas to the value of another mineral water that they possessed in vast quantities – the sea itself. Doctors began to advocate the health giving properties of cold sea water baths. In 1702 Sir John Floyer, an eminent and respected physician brought out a book which pointed out to its readers, that 'since we live on an island, and have the sea about us, we cannot want for an excellent cold bath, which will both preserve our healths and cure many diseases – ulcers, scabs, scaled heads, itching and leprous corns, tumours, pains of the limbs, hydrophobia, all inflammations, all catharral effects, nephritis, gonorrhea, arthritis etc.' His faithful followers began – gingerly no doubt – to try out the efficacy of his treatment, and spurred by the traditional British illusion that anything unpleasant must of necessity be beneficial, they committed themselves with upper lips stiff with determination, if not with cold, to the uninviting grey seas.

The Rigours of 'The Dip'

They were unlikely to have enjoyed the experience. Despite the encouragement of Sir John, there probably still lurked at the back of their minds the suspicion that any benefits from the bracing sea water would be cancelled out by the dangerous 'saline effluvia' – the damp invisible miasma which many people still believed to hang over the ocean, and to cause all sorts of minor ailments. Their bodies were certainly blue with cold; for it was believed that bathing was only safe when the pores of one's skin were firmly closed – therefore one must choose a day when the sea and the weather were both thoroughly chilly. This is why we read in the diaries of the time of visitors going to the seaside in November rather than in the Summer, when the body was heated to a dangerous degree, and the pores were wide open to all sorts of nameless infections. There was also another problem which caused considerable anxiety – that of getting into the water. From Setterington's famous engraving of Scarborough it seems that some self-assured eighteenth-century gentlemen merely strode naked and unashamed into the water where they splashed about in full view of any interested onlookers. This was not, however, considered a seemly procedure for ladies, and there were a number of less inhibited gentlemen who also looked for a way of ensuring a greater degree of modesty. The problem was partially solved by the invention of the bathing machine. Prospective bathers would go down to the beach to one of several 'bathing rooms' where their names would be called out as the machines became vacant. They would then get into a small wooden cabin on wheels, and be pulled by a horse far enough out to sea to give them the privacy they craved – though gentlemen with telescopes can often be detected in contemporary engravings, hopefully stationed on the shore.

On reaching a point in the water deep enough for a really thorough soaking,

24   Fishing villages like Scarborough grew into well-known resorts.

25 The Steyne at Brighton. The lady in black on the left is Martha Gunn, a well-known dipper. The gentleman on the black horse is the Prince Regent. The domed house in the background is the Pavilion as it was before the Prince's alterations.

the shivering victim would open the door of the machine, to be greeted by one of the brawny 'dippers' who were stationed in the waves at many of the new resorts. Many of these were women who were accustomed to stand voluminously clothed in a rough sea for three or four hours at a time. They grasped their clients firmly and held them giggling or indeed sometimes shrieking, against the waves. The most famous of these dippers were Martha Gunn and Old Smoaker at Brighton. Old Smoaker was a male dipper, and a particular favourite of the Prince Regent. On one occasion when the Prince himself was being dipped he had very foolishly ventured further into the rough sea than Old Smoaker considered safe. When his stern shouts of warning were ignored by his prince, Old Smoaker firmly seized him by the ear and dragged him back to safety. Happily, the Prince is said to have taken this peremptory treatment with unruffled good humour, continued to employ Old Smoaker and awarded him a pension on his retirement. Some resorts deplored the tough treatment meted out by the dippers, and tried in their advertisements to project a more attractive image. One of the lady dippers at Margate proclaimed her 'skill and tenderness', and the corporation announced that their dippers were in general 'very pretty and well behaved young women, very different from the clumsy old women guides at Brighthelmstone (Brighton)'.

Even though the lady bathers were usually attired in tent-like garments during their dip many of them were still worried at being seen too closely by inquisitive gentlemen bathers. They were further embarrassed that those gentlemen bathers who defied the notice boards urging strict segregation, and ventured too near, were often naked. This problem was to be solved to a certain extent in the nineteenth century, partly by stricter segregation and partly by the ingenious invention of a Quaker gentleman named Benjamin Beale, of the modesty hood. This was an expanding canvas hood, rather like an elongated version of a pram hood, which was attached to the lady's bathing machine, and which for the moment when she stepped into the sea, was pulled down to water-level. The lady could thus take her dip in conditions 'consistent with the most refined delicacy' – also one would imagine in complete and claustrophobic darkness! It was not until the later years of the nineteenth century that the problem was to be finally solved when English gentlemen at last adopted a custom practised in all other civilised countries of Europe, the wearing of bathing drawers or calecons.

During the eighteenth century, sea bathing was put firmly into a medical context, and was taken extremely seriously. No one suggested that the whole thing might be a bit of a lark. All sorts of precautions were taken to make sure that the treatment would be thoroughly effective, like making sure that the towel used for drying had itself been rinsed out in sea water, so ensuring that all the valuable mineral deposits possible were left on one's skin. A more troublesome practice was that of making sure that the bowels were empty before one entered the sea. The purge used was sea water, of course, taken in great quantities – sometimes as much as four pints a day – mixed with milk for those of a delicate constitution. For the poor unfortunates who could not get to the seaside, various enterprising merchants bottled the water and sold it in the London shops.

The location of the first resorts
Not all the little fishing ports of England became fashionable resorts overnight. By the end of the eighteenth century there were still only a handful of places that could be said to be firmly established with a regular clientele of faithful visitors. After all the population of Britain was still only 11 million and there were few of them who could yet afford to take a holiday every year. Though the road system was by now developing briskly there were still many hundreds of square miles especially along the sea coast that were completely out of reach. Many of the most beautiful areas like Cornwall could only be reached after an uncomfortable journey of several days from the main towns and cities. It was indeed because of this remoteness that such areas were able to preserve their character and beauty until the early years of this present century.

The seaside villages that were first transformed into resorts were all relatively easy to reach. Many of the Sussex and Kent resorts were within a few hours journey from London. Scarborough and Whitby were accessible to the Yorkshire woollen merchants and manufacturers. Lyme Regis owed its popularity with a select group of visitors to the fact that in 1757 its steep high street was linked with the main London to Exeter road.

26 The trip to Margate became increasingly popular.

MARGATE PASSAGE PACKET.

The ROBERT and JANE,
R. KIDD, MASTER,
Being fitted up in a very commodious Manner,
SAILS during the Summer Season, with Passengers and Baggage, from MARGATE every Monday, and from DICE KEY, near Billingsgate, London, every Thursday.
The GREAT CABIN, 5s. each Passenger, has 16 Beds—One Bed, when Numbers require it, may be possess'd alternately by 4 Persons.
The MIDDLE CABIN, 7s. each Passenger, has 6 Beds—One Bed, when Numbers require it, may be possess'd alternately by 3 Persons.
The AFTER CABIN, has Two Beds, and may be hired by Four Persons, at 10s. 6d. each.
All Goods and Parcels forwarded with the greatest Care and Dispatch; but the Master will be answerable for those only delivered into his Care to pay Freight. Children in Arms, Half Price.
Passengers to pay Half Price when Places are taken.
Jewels, Plate, and Money, will not be accounted for, unless paid as such.

The Rise of Margate

One popular resort whose popularity was not dependent on roads but on water transport, was Margate. It did not cost much to get there from London, and so it was one of the first towns to offer seaside pleasures to ordinary people. In the days before reliably surfaced roads were built, the quickest and therefore the cheapest way of transporting goods was by water. The seamen of Margate, as their fishing industry declined, turned for a living to the Thames, as a reasonably quick route to London. They used one-masted sailing ships or 'hoys' for their journey, and on these loaded their cargoes of corn to supply the London merchants. On their return journey they loaded up not only with goods for the shopkeepers at home, but with Londoners wanting a breath of sea air and a sight of the coast. For half a crown the passengers took their chance – of a quick nine-hour trip in a good wind, or of a three-day buffeting if the weather was against them. By the end of the eighteenth century 18,000 visitors a year were being deposited on Margate's prospering jetty. The crews of the hoys seem to have taken to their human cargoes with little trouble, and as Charles Lamb records in his essay 'The Old Margate Hoy', they answered their passengers' questions, and ministered to the seasick ones with unfailing good humour. Margate responded with delight to this new source of wealth, though her more aristocratic visitors, for whom the Assembly

Rooms had originally been built, were taken aback to find that the Parade where they walked, the Theatre Royal and the libraries were becoming increasingly crowded with cheerful and noisy Londoners determined to enjoy themselves. The citizens of Margate, though insisting on decorous behaviour on the hoys as well as in the town itself, welcomed them all with pleasure. In a truly generous spirit, they founded a hospital where poor people could take a sea water cure for their ailments. It was to this hospital that the poor friendless, scrofulous youth whom Charles Lamb met on the hoy, was going in hopes of a cure.

King George III at Weymouth
Other seaside towns owed their prosperity, not to the visits of the humble, but to the patronage of the rich, the aristocracy and above all the royal family. The last years of King George III's life were shadowed by recurring attacks of madness. The remedies prescribed for him were those of an age which understood nothing of the causes or the cures for mental illness. Most of the treatment recommended by the King's physicians was brutal as well as ineffective. Fortunately for the poor king, sea bathing as well as whipping and confinement was thought to be helpful in the treatment of insanity, and after his first attack in 1789, George decided to go to Weymouth, a quiet, respectable, little town were he was assured of a restful routine. We know he enjoyed his visit, for Fanny Burney, the writer, was lady in waiting to Queen Charlotte at the time, and she recorded her impressions of the visit in detail. It was not exactly a quiet visit; the townsfolk of Weymouth were far too delighted with their illustrious visitor to leave him entirely alone. They cheered respectfully as the distinguished monarch descended from his bathing machine, and stood solemnly to attention while the town band struck up the National Anthem to accompany the King's bathe. Whenever he took an evening stroll, 'an immense crowd attended him – sailors, bargemen, mechanics, countrymen; and all united in so vociferous a volley of "God Save the King" that the noise was stunning.' To the delight and relief of the people 'The pure air of Weymouth had a visible effect on the health of our beloved sovereign.' The short term effects on the prosperity of the town were negligible for the King spent as little money as possible. He was a careful man and preferred to import supplies from the Home Farm at Windsor.

> Bread, chees, salt, catchup, vinegar and mustard;
> Small beer and bacon, apple pye and custard;
> All, all from Windsor greets his frugal grace,
> For Weymouth is a d-mned expensive place.

However, the long term effects of the King's favour on Weymouth's popularity more than made up for the King's parsimony. His affection for the town remained constant throughout the rest of his life, and the regular visits he made there were one of the few pleasures left to him during a tragic old age.

27 Fashionable resorts like Weymouth provided at least one hotel for wealthy visitors.

The Prince at Brighton

One of the reasons that King George chose to patronise Weymouth was his anxiety to avoid Brighton at all costs. King George liked and needed a quiet life, and he knew that this was not to be found in a town where both his brother, the Duke of Gloucester, and his son, the Prince of Wales, indulged their taste for gay society and high life. Brighton's rise to the position of Queen of English resorts is often attributed solely to the patronage of the Prince Regent, but Brighton – originally Brighthelmstone – was a small but successful resort, with a loyal and well-bred clientele before ever the Prince had visited it. London families found the sixty-mile drive there preferable to the long uncomfortable journey to Bath. Brighton, they found, had all the convenience of Tunbridge Wells with the added benefits of sea water bathing. They even convinced themselves that its austere treeless cliffs were particularly healthy, being so delightfully free of the 'noxious fumes of perspiring trees'. It was these visitors who gave Brighton her initial success. Some of them were not at all pleased by the arrival of an extrovert, pleasure-loving

28 *The Old Chain Pier at Brighton.* A painting by John Constable.

29 The Pavilion at Brighton – after the alterations.

prince to disturb their pleasant and decorous routine. Many of them withdrew their patronage and departed to other south coast resorts whose even tenor had not been disrupted by rumbustious royalty.

Certainly after the first visit of the Prince in 1783 Brighton was never quite the same again. The Prince unlike his father was not interested in a quiet life, and under his patronage the Brighton season became one of the gayest gatherings in Europe. As the *Morning Post* observed in July 1785, 'Morning rides, champagne, dissipation, noise and nonsense, jumble these phrases together and you have a complete account of all that's passing in Brightelmstone.' In the centre of it all arose the Prince's beloved Pavilion – originally a pretty, elegant house belonging to a Mr Thomas Kemp. Over thirty years of its new royal owner's unremitting enthusiasm for exotic architectural flourishes it became a formidable collection of pinnacles and domes until taken over by the architect John Nash who gave it some kind of exterior unity. Its unexpected onion domes and oriental appearance still dominate Brighton today and remind us of the noisy gaiety of an age that for some people was even more permissive than our own. As the Prince Regent's visits to Brighton became more and more prolonged, fashionable London society began its series of yearly migrations. By the end of the eighteenth century its permanent population had more than doubled with the influx of builders, servants, milliners, dressmakers and shopkeepers who came to profit from the new opportunities provided by Brighton's aristocratic visitors. Whole squares and terraces of handsome houses were built, for in those days gentlemen of fashion preferred to take a house for the season so that they could ensure the standards of service and comfort to which they were accustomed.

Eighteenth-century Travel

This growth of readiness to take up residence away from home whether at Bath or Brighton, Buxton or Bridlington should be set against the background of the rapidly developing transport system of late eighteenth-century England. People were only prepared to move away from home for a holiday if they knew that they could travel in reasonable comfort. When journeys, however delightful the destination, were likely to lead over undrained roads, where highwaymen lurked in the cover of uncleared forests, most people even the wealthy ones preferred to stay at home. But as the turnpike trusts took over more and more roads, renewing their surfaces, and paying officials to supervise them, more and more people were inclined to venture on longer journeys, and to regard them as diversions rather than as endurance tests. This growing traffic on the roads in its turn played its part in stimulating even more turnpike trusts and in providing more funds for further road building.

Improvements in transport, convenience of location, the search for health, the whims of fashion, all combined in the development of the English seaside resort. By the end of the century the idea of a holiday by the sea had for the first time become a commonplace for at least a proportion of the population.

And along with the horrid drinks of sea water, the rigours of the dip, the pleasures of the fashionable life, was growing the realisation that the seaside was a pleasant even a beautiful place to be. The stage was set for the nineteenth-century expansion of seaside development and the opening up of the coastal resorts to a new and livelier public.

30 The Turnpike at Tottenham Court Road, 1813.

5 I Do Like to be beside the Sea

The citizens of the newly favoured seaside towns might congratulate themselves on their increasing trade and custom; little did they realize that by the end of the nineteenth century, they would have a share in a booming tourist industry, and that small towns would have been quickly transformed into prosperous boroughs with large resident populations, and throngs of summer visitors drawn from all classes of society.

Yet in the first decades of the century, seaside holidays remained the prerogative of the rich. At that time they alone had the two commodities which make holidays possible – leisure and surplus cash. Only those with money could afford to buy the comfort which made a long journey tolerable. The roads had certainly been improved, but the jolting and stuffiness of the stage coaches were such as to daunt any but the most determined traveller. As William Cobbett observed with characteristic trenchancy, 'To travel by ordinary stage coach is to be hurried along by force in a box with an air hole in it, and constantly exposed to broken limbs, the danger being much greater than that on shipboard, and the noise much more disagreeable, while the company is frequently not a great deal to one's liking.' Most people, unable to afford their own well-sprung carriages, and without regular holidays, stayed at home; and the seaside resorts in those years

31 A Toll Gate. The money paid by the travellers went to improve the existing roads and build new ones.

32 Travelling carriages became more elegant and more comfortable.

before Victoria became Queen, remained the preserves of the rich and the gently born.

Something of that old elegant past still lingers in the Regency buildings and quiet corners of our older coastal towns; but over the years of the nineteenth century that calm and seclusion which had appealed to well-bred visitors was to be largely eroded. The upper classes, increasingly jostled against tradespeople, clerks and even factory workers, gradually withdrew their patronage as a new, and in some respects, noisier public discovered the delights of the sea.

A Revolution in Transport

It all began as so many things in Victorian England did, with the power of steam. It was the discovery of steam power in the eighteenth century that had set the wheels and machinery of England's Industrial Revolution turning. The nineteenth century was to see that power applied to transportation, not only of goods but of human beings. By 1815 pleasure steamers were cruising down the Clyde, and by the 1820s steam boats had taken the place of the old Margate hoys. People living on the West coast now found that the Isle of Man was within their reach, and so established it for the first time as a popular resort particularly for the people of Lancashire. There were occasional complaints about the noise and vibration, but these were small matters, compared with the speed, cheapness and safety of the journey. It now took only a more or less guaranteed eight hours to travel from London to Margate, and by 1835, the Margate Pier and Harbour Company was carrying 105,625 passengers a year. The Londoner on his rare days out could now also take a steamer to Southend for a return fare of three shillings or to Deal for six shillings.

The possibility of a quick trip in a steam boat was a delightful and liberating development for those people who lived near the harbours and ports from which they sailed. Most British people, however, lived inland. It was the fast growing railway system and steam locomotives that were to give them new opportunities to get out of their often grim surroundings, if only for a few hours.

The Coming of the Railways

The original enthusiasm for steam-powered railway transport came first of all from the great industrial interests. The coal to drive the engines was cheap, and the railways were able to cope efficiently and speedily with bulky raw materials and with crates of manufactured goods. From the beginning, however, railway entrepreneurs and the public at large realised that here was a way of connecting not only factories and ports and markets, but people and places too. By 1851 seven thousand miles of track had been laid, the great main lines had been completed, and 80 million passengers a year were travelling by train. Sometimes the journeys were negligible in our present day terms. Nevertheless the coming of the railways marked the beginning of the end of the long era when most British people lived out their lives within an area of a few square miles. 'I rejoice to see it,' said Dr Arnold 'and rejoice to see that the old feudality is gone for ever.' By 1890 the railways were carrying 817,000,000 passengers a year.

Year by year more routes were built linking the inland cities of Britain with the sea. This development was ultimately to shatter the upper-class calm of the seaside resorts, as more and more people were able to avail themselves of the new services. At first, however, the poorer classes were still firmly tied to their workaday world by lack of money and free time. It was the middle class that was to be the first beneficiary. This was the class that in the nineteenth century was constantly

33 *Seaford in Sussex.* This painting by Walter Collins suggests the spaciousness and remoteness of the seaside before the railway came.

growing in size and influence, as Britain's expanding industry and commerce opened up new jobs, and as power shifted from the old aristocratic land-owning class to the industrialists, financiers and lawyers. When these bankers, managers, factory owners took a train journey they were pleased to find the superior comfort suitable to their station, and had no hesitation in allowing their wives and children to board the well sprung, luxuriously padded carriages. Charles Greville, the diarist, spoke for his contemporaries when he recorded, with slightly surprised pleasure, this first train journey – 'Nothing can be more comfortable than the vehicle in which I was put, a sort of chariot with two places, and there is nothing disagreeable about it except the whiffs of stinking air which it is impossible to exclude altogether. The first sensation is a slight degree of nervousness and a feeling of being run away with but a sense of security supervenes and the velocity is delightful. Town after town, one park and chateau after another are left behind with the rapid velocity of a moving panorama, and the continual bustle and animation of the changes and stoppages made the journey very entertaining. . . . Considering the novelty of its establishment, there is very little embarrassment, and it entirely renders all other travelling irksome and tedious by comparison.' As long journeys became bearable, even enjoyable, a few days away from home for a breath of sea air became more and more of a commonplace.

The Seaside Holiday
This new passion for moving about unnecessarily caused some head-shaking. As *The Times* observed in one of its leaders 'Among those who are well-to-do the annual trip to the seaside has become a necessity of which their fathers, or at least their grandfathers never dreamt.'

Sometimes, however, that 'annual trip' had a motive which other generations would certainly have understood – the search for health. The idea that sea water bathing and sea air were beneficial still persisted triumphantly, and it was a belief that was particularly reassuring in an age which, because of over burdened drainage and uncertain water supplies, was pathetically vulnerable to disease. It is now that children begin to appear in the water colours and sketches of seaside scenes. Brought by anxious parents to convalesce after bouts of infectious illness, they found the treatment greatly to their taste. Although impeded by the thick clothes which the Victorians thought indispensable for all seasons of the year, they embarked happily on the shell collecting, paddling and general bucket and spade activities that still delight their more blasé and scantily clad great-great-grandchildren.

For some children and for some grown ups the search for health was sadly unavailing. Too many of them were suffering from serious diseases – particularly from tuberculosis – for which there was as yet no cure. Yet they still went on hoping that somehow the fresh air by the sea would bring back health and vigour. Anne Brontë wrote bravely to her sister, 'The doctors say that a change of air or

34 At first only the middle classes could afford seaside holidays. They still used bathing machines for 'dipping'.

removal to a better climate would hardly ever fail in consumptive cases, if the remedy were taken in time.' It was this advice that impelled her to take her last sad journey from Haworth to Scarborough, so that she could drive on the sands and sit out in a sheltered spot on the beach. For her as for so many of her contemporaries the seaside holiday brought no cure and she died four days after leaving her home.

For the majority of middle-class visitors, however, the holiday habit was wholly beneficial. They were able to take long bracing walks along the cliffs, and to enjoy the company of their children in a rather more relaxed atmosphere than that usually prevailing in Victorian households.

Problems of Segregation

One pastime, however, that the family could not enjoy together was bathing, for until the end of the century, segregation was strictly enforced. At Southport any pleasure boat approaching the ladies' bathing area was fined five shillings, and

35 Bobbing up and down at the end of a rope was the Victorian's idea of seabathing.

the gentlemen's bathing machines were firmly kept at a distance of at least a hundred yards. There is some evidence to suggest that opera glasses and telescopes were a common item of equipment for many gentlemen taking a seaside holiday. The main reason for this strictly enforced segregation was that quite late into the century many gentlemen obstinately persisted in the habit of bathing naked. They disliked the bathing drawers or calecons affected by more modest young men, and thought them unnatural if not positively dangerous. One young curate called Francis Kilvert seems to have been particularly disgusted at the whole idea. While on holiday at Shanklin in 1874, he observed in his diary, 'At Shanklin one has to adopt the detestable custom of bathing in drawers. If ladies don't like to see men naked, why don't they keep away from the sight?... To-day I had a pair of drawers given me which I could not keep on. The rough waves stripped them off and tore them down round my ankles. While thus fettered I was seized and flung down in a heavy sea which retreating suddenly left me lying naked on the sharp shingle from which I rose streaming with blood.' The woman and girls went to the other extreme; they were so used to their normal layers of cambric, and flannel that it took a considerable amount of clothing to make them feel really

36 The Victorians did not copy their eighteenth-century forbears and bathe naked. They preferred to be well – though elegantly – covered.

secure before they entered the water. In the early days of the seaside holiday they enveloped themselves in long flannel tents, but as these garments merely floated on the surface of the water leaving most of their bodies exposed, they did not fulfil the requirements of the typical Victorian woman. They felt more comfortable in a good thick pair of pantaloons, teamed with dresses made of stockingette or serge, and elaborately tucked, frilled and braided. The ironic thing was that as these fearsome garments clung closely to the figure when wet, they were, in fact, far less discreet than some of our modern bathing oufits. Over the years Victorian ladies became aware of this disturbing tendency of their bathing dresses to reveal all – and added corsets to their already overburdened forms. In the eighties there was a temporary fashion for one piece outfits – not really as daring as they sound for they covered the body thoroughly from neck to knee, and long serge stockings took over where the bathing suit left off! It was perhaps just as well that impeded as they must have been, they had not yet acquired a taste for swimming. They much preferred 'bobbing up and down in shallow water at the end of a rope'.

Victorian summers, then, saw the bulk of the middle-class population of Britain firmly established with their children, nannies and shrimping nets, beside the sea. It took many more years before the lower paid workers joined them and a more complex set of circumstances.

Working-Class Conditions

The Industrial Revolution brought in the long term great prosperity and a higher standard of living to all sections of the community. For the majority of industrial workers the short term effects of their migration from agriculture to industry were depressing, and they were to wait many years before the conditions they endured brought them anything like an adequate reward. The nineteenth-century industrial city, which mushroomed into existence before anyone had really had time to think about it was a thoroughly unpleasant place to live in – dirty, ugly and overcrowded. Men, women and children worked long hours for low wages on dangerous machinery. Their diet was poor, their housing inadequate, and there seemed in the early years of the century little hope of relief. Few people can have been more in need of a holiday nor less able to take one.

Not only could they not afford transport, but in those days regular days off work even without pay were, (except for the workers of Lancashire who still were allowed their traditional 'wakes weeks') unknown. Factory owners who had risked their capital to set up expensive machinery wanted to keep that machinery working. Unless they made a profit they knew they were finished, and they also knew that their profit was dependent on the labour of their work people, for whom, however, they spared little sympathy. This was a tense period in industrial relations; employers were not yet experienced enough or sure enough of their success to relax into tolerance or compassion for their workers' problems. It was easier for them to condemn their employees as a drunken idle lot, than to analyse the reasons for their frequent absenteeism. 'I have not the least doubt,' said one Staffordshire employer, 'but that I should prosper greatly if I could depend on the working hours of the men. They often come about the premises but will not buckle to. If I give them a day or two at Easter they take a week, if at Christmas, they take another week; indeed they are not to be depended upon.' It occurred to very few employers that better working conditions might bring a more co-operative response, and that increased opportunities for leisure might result in a working class who no longer needed to find oblivion from their troubles in drink.

The determined self interest of many employers had combined with Victorian religious ideas, to take away the few opportunities for leisure and enjoyment still open to the working classes. The old sports of bull and bear fighting, cock fighting and prize fights were understandably attacked by middle-class writers and politicians as brutal and degraded. By 1840 all these sports were illegal, but no alternative forms of entertainment had been provided. Moreover, the traditional holy days which had for so long helped to cheer the monotony of the working year had been gradually whittled away, first by the Puritan influences of the seventeenth century, later by the irresistible combination of the Victorians' distrust of idleness, especially among their social inferiors, and their equally strong disapproval of the lingering remnants of paganism.

There were, nevertheless, even in the tough conditions of the first half of the century, some employers who took a more benevolent attitude. In Lancashire the old tradition of 'wakes weeks' – which had probably originated in a week being set aside for the spreading of fresh rushes on the floor – was left untouched. In Manchester crowds of people were able to flock to Kersal Moor for the four days of Whitsuntide horse racing, and Lancashire mill workers were able to get to the seaside much earlier than those in other areas.

It must be remembered, too, that most workers accepted unquestioningly their employers' niggardly attitude to holidays. Their unions had other more pressing improvements to battle for, and in any case, working people of those days had very little idea of how enjoyable it could be to spend a holiday 'rationally' – a favourite middle-class expression of the day. They were imprisoned not only by lack of cheap transport and leisure time but also by minds cramped by miserable living conditions.

The Beginning of Working-Class Holidays
The second half of the century was to see a considerable lightening of this gloomy picture. By then Britain was secure in her position as the greatest trading nation in the world with immense industrial power and assured markets for her goods in every continent. A new climate of confidence, a conviction that the future was going to be even better, helped to relax many employers into a more enlightened and humane attitude to their work people. They noticed that in factories where time off was fairly generously allowed, there seemed to be no corresponding fall in

production. Indeed in some instances absenteeism decreased and there was a greater will to work.

The Factory Act of 1850 gave official expression to this more liberal attitude. No young persons or women were allowed to work after 2 pm on Saturdays, and as there was no point in keeping the looms and machinery operating with only half the labour force present, most factories sent everybody home. In 1871 the ready acceptance of the Bank Holiday Act also partly reflected this more relaxed atmosphere, though it also reflected a lack of understanding of its full implications for all British workers. Holidays were fixed not just for the usual times of Christmas, Whitsun and Easter but for a new August holiday that was to be taken on the first Monday of that month. After only a year, the new holiday was happily established. Factories, shops and offices were firmly closed, and as the *Daily News* commented, 'How much such a day of relaxation is needed, its universal acceptance proves'.

Cheap Railway Travel
In the early years of their history the railways had seemed to offer little to the poorer classes of society. Third-class travel was not only dear but excruciatingly uncomfortable, in carriages that were no better than cattle trucks. In 1844, however, the Select Committee on Railways recommended a penny a mile fare and an improvement in second- and third-class accommodation. Carriages were

37 Third-class travel was uncomfortable but it could be fun. This picture is taken from a Victorian song sheet.

now enclosed, provided with windows and ventilation and passengers on all sections of a train were given a much smoother ride on the spring buffers that were introduced in the 1840s. More significant still were the cheap excursion rates which the main railway companies introduced. People who had never moved more than a few miles from home before rushed to buy their tickets. In 1845 the excursion trains from Manchester on Whit Monday carried 15,000 people. Choirs, Sunday schools and temperance societies became quite accustomed to chartering whole trains for their members. Entrepreneurs like Mr Thomas Cook began to hire trains at their own risk, and offer the tickets for sale at reduced yet still profitable rates. Most of his early ventures were organized for temperance societies but in 1845 he offered accommodation to the general public, on an excursion from Leicester, Nottingham and Derby to Liverpool for 10s to 14s with a trip to Caernarvon and Snowdon available at an extra charge.

The convenience and cheapness of the railways, the increased leisure time would have been of little use to the working classes without the increase in real wages that resulted from Britain's growing prosperity. At last work people were finding that industrialisation was benefiting them as well as their employers. Wages were higher, food and clothing was cheaper and their standard of living improved. At last they had a little money to spare, and at least a limited amount of travel was within their reach.

A dramatic symbol of this growing mobility of all classes, as well of Britain's increasing wealth and economic power was provided by the Great Exhibition of 1851. Thousands of manufactured goods from pen knives to locomotives were on display to the world and no doubt equally impressive to the foreign visitor were the millions of people from the provinces who were able to afford the fare to come and admire the impressive display that they had helped to make possible. As one writer of the day expressed it, 'The state of the Metropolis throughout the whole period of the Great Exhibition will be remembered with wonder and admiration by all. . . . Instead of confusion, disorder, and demoralisation if not actual revolution, which were predicted by some gloomy minds. . . . London exhibited a great degree of order, good-humoured accommodation of her crowds, and power to provide for their wants. . . . Enormous excursion trains daily poured their thousands. . . . It was like a gigantic picnic . . . large numbers of work people received holidays for the purpose. . . . 800 agricultural labourers in their peasants' attire from Surrey and Sussex, conducted by the clergy at a cost of two and two-pence each person – numerous firms in the North sent their people, who must have been gratified by the sight of their own handiwork.'

Even after the exhibition was over many excursions were organised to similar if slightly less momentous occasions. Savings clubs were started so that families could save up for a trip to a concert or festival. The most common destination of all, however, was the sea.

Now that they could afford the fare people in most industrial and market towns of Britain found that the railways had linked them with the coast. The seaside

38 The Pier became an indispensable feature of every sizeable seaside resort.

towns and villages of North and South Wales, Somerset, Lancashire, Devon and Hampshire as well as the older resorts were now accessible and therefore ripe for development. Some towns like Bournemouth still geared their rapidly expanding facilities and accommodation to the middle and upper classes; many others realised that there was money to be made from the day trippers from the cities.

Holiday Pleasures

This new public did not want to spend precious holiday times in sedate middle-class amusements. They wanted entertainment, company and noise, and as there was money to be made out of giving them what they wanted, the more genteel visitors protested in vain. The new piers which many resorts had built, gave them considerable scope for entertainment. These well-known seaside structures were originally landing jetties. It was the far-sighted folk of Brighton who had first seen their commercial possibilities. By 1824 any visitor to Brighton could walk safely out to sea on the reassuringly solid pier and enjoy not only the sea breezes but also a glass of mineral water or a visit to the 'camera obscura'. In 1839 he could indulge himself in the further diversion of actually weighing himself on a newly imported machine. As the booming seaside towns competed for their customers they vied with one another in providing more and more shops, peep shows and slot machines along their piers. There was plenty of music too on the piers and in the parks and promenades. Mrs Carlyle complained that at Ramsgate, 'A brass band plays all through breakfast and repeats the performance often during the day.' Picture postcards, rock, ice cream, fish and chips, funny hats and cheap souvenirs all contributed to the fun of a good day out and brought huge profits to their suppliers.

Towards the end of the century the gradual rise in real wages meant that some people could contemplate spending a whole week by the sea. The Lancashire cotton workers with their long established 'wakes weeks' were among the first to be able to enjoy this new opportunity; Blackpool was consequently one of the first towns to see the rise of the landlady and her boarding house to a position of great significance in working-class life. More and more resorts followed the example of Lancashire and began to offer clean and well kept accommodation at reasonable prices. Sometimes families who could not afford full board, provided their own food with the landlady acting as cook. Whatever the arrangement it was a break from routine that would scarcely have been dreamt of at the beginning of the century.

For many thousands of ordinary people at the end of the century the world was at last stable and assured with the promise of even better things to come; but there were still countless others who remained imprisoned by their poverty.

39 Blackpool in 1895.

There were still people particularly in the country areas who lived out their lives within the old circumscribed traditions and within a few square miles. Thousands of families throughout Britain were still too poor to afford even a cheap fare to fresh air and a sight of the sea.

It was a measure of the growing compassion of the times and of the new emphasis on the benefits of a seaside holiday for all that the first charities were set up at the end of the century to pay for poor children to get away from the slums for a week by the sea. Many appeals were made and many middle-class Victorians were quick to respond. An annual holiday which had once been thought of as a privilege only for the wealthy was now on its way to being regarded as a necessity, almost as a right.

6 In Search of Beauty

As the eighteenth century drew to a close many people for the first time were beginning to discover the pleasures of landscape and the charms of beautiful and impressive scenery. Painters and poets throughout Europe – Claude, Corot, Gainsborough, Wordsworth, Coleridge, Keats and many others were deriving their inspiration from all aspects of Nature. They were no longer repelled as their forbears had often been by wild moorland and towering mountains; rather did they enjoy their scale and grandeur. At the same time they took pleasure in the less awe-inspiring pleasures of the countryside and, influenced by the writings of naturalists like Gilbert White of Selborne, spent much time in detailed observation of animals and flowers.

Country Pleasures

This new awareness of landscape permeates the painting and writing of the period. Even as early as 1736 the Reverend William Clarke had written while on holiday

40 *Gordale Scar* by James Ward. At the beginning of the nineteenth century people were beginning to lose their fear of wild mountain scenery and regard it as romantic.

41 Artists and writers liked to find quiet seaside villages away from the crowds.

at Brighton, 'We are now sunning ourselves upon the beach at Brightelmstone. Such a tract of sea, such regions of corn ... My morning business is bathing in the sea, and then buying fish: the evening is riding out for air, viewing the remains of the old Saxon camps.' No mention there of his health, or taking a cure – just enjoyment of the sun and the sea and a glimpse of History. Jane Austen, in her novel *Persuasion* gives the Musgrove family a lively appreciation of the picturesque setting of Lyme Regis and they never once mention its medical advantages. Elizabeth Bennett in *Pride and Prejudice* surveys the park at Pemberley with a sharp, discerning eye. 'Every disposition of the ground was good; and she looked at the whole scene, the river, the trees scattered on its banks, and the winding of the valley, as far as she could trace it, with delight.' The sentence typifies a lively response to beauty, though a controlled and ladylike one. An amusing contrast is to be found in a description of Charlotte Brontë's reaction to her first sight of the sea at Bridlington, which shows a more thoroughgoing romantic sensibility. 'She was quite overpowered, she could not speak till she had shed some tears, – she signed to a friend to leave her and walk on; this she did for a few steps, knowing full well what Charlotte was passing through and the stern efforts she was making to subdue her emotions – her friend joined her as soon as she might without inflicting pain; her eyes were red and swollen, she was still trembling, but submitted to being led towards where the view was less impressive'.

Whichever way it took you this eagerness to respond to beautiful scenery became an important element in nineteenth-century holidays, and was to bring visitors to hitherto remote parts of Britain. Even before the railways came intrepid tourists were making their way on horseback, on donkeys, sometimes even on foot, over the passes that would lead them into the mountains of Wales and of the Lake District.

Scotland too could offer all the grandeur and contrast of scenery that delighted Victorian travellers. Even the mists and lowering clouds did not deter them, for these were so often a feature of the paintings and the literature which they admired. Moreover, Scotland could offer not only mountains and lakes, but places charged with literary and historical associations. Most eminent of all the lovers of Scotland was of course Queen Victoria herself. Some of the happiest times of her life were spent at Balmoral, the Deeside home which she and Prince Albert had had built and decorated to their own taste. She loved the scenery and the solitude. 'It was wonderful,' she wrote, 'not seeing a single human being, nor hearing a sound except that of the wind, or the call of the blackcock or grouse.' She was speaking, too, for many of her subjects who were coming to favour the quiet pleasures of a

42 Queen Victoria and her husband Prince Albert enjoyed the wild scenery and the remoteness of the Scottish Highlands.

country holiday. She also liked to be able to quote her favourite author, Sir Walter Scott, amid the scenery of his novels and she enjoyed the novelty and colour of Scottish customs and traditions. The Prince, with his usual application, tried to learn Gaelic, his children learned Scottish dances and he and his wife conceived a passion for tartan as the interior decoration of Balmoral still shows. Indeed if we are to believe certain witnesses the Queen in her later years went so far in her uncritical approval of all things Scottish that she acquired the taste for 'a wee dram' of whisky in her tea.

Foreign Travel
This quest for the strange and the beautiful led the well-off tourist not only to the remote parts of Britain, but also to the Continent, and strengthened the taste for foreign travel that had originally developed among the aristocracy as a legacy of the Grand Tour. Disenchanted with the seaside resorts which were by now increasingly being invaded by tradespeople and factory workers the upper classes began to travel abroad in search of more congenial society as well as impressive scenery.

Where the aristocracy led the middle classes of course followed. This was the beginning of Switzerland's popularity with the English tourist, for it satisfied more

43 Turner's painting of Venice, *The Bridge of Sighs*. This was the sort of picture that sharpened the nineteenth-century taste for travel.

44 A party of early nineteenth-century travellers enjoy the thrill as well as the grandeur of Swiss mountain scenery.

than anywhere else the passion for remote mountain scenery that had become such an important part of current English taste. Frederick Harrison, an early visitor, captured something of this when he recorded his own delight, 'I was carried out of all good sense and self-control by the fascination of this new transcendent world. I deserted my friends and comrades, I raced about the crags and rattled down the snow glissades, tramped throught the night, rose to see the dawn in midsummer, and behaved like a youth in a state of delirium.' In the first half of the century most visitors preferred to look at the mountains rather than to climb them, and the first major resorts developed in the valleys and by the lakesides. In the 1850s however more and more people began to see the mountains as a challenge to bodies made flabby by long periods of inactivity, and the great sport of mountaineering was born. The Alpine Club was established and an increasing number of enthusiasts began to learn the skills of Alpine climbing.

Switzerland's development as a tourist resort was also partly due to her healthy mountain air. Doctors increasingly advised their well off patients with tuberculosis to visit the Swiss mountains where the progress of the disease was often halted

45 The Riviera became a favourite holiday playground for the rich.

sometimes for many years by breathing in the pure atmosphere, and leading the rigorously healthy life advocated by specialists in lung diseases like Switzerland's Doctor Brehmer. These visitors came not in summer with the normal holiday makers but in winter, and little mountain villages like Davos and Andermatt found themselves prospering from a year-round season. They also found that visitors were increasingly coming not only to visit patients in the nearby sanatoria but to enjoy the fun of skating and tobogganing in the crisp dry air, often warmed by the sunshine so rare during an English winter. These winter sports became even more popular with British tourists when skiing, originally a Norwegian sport, was introduced towards the end of the century by a few fanatical English skiers like Arnold Lunn, E. C. Richardson and Vivian Caulfield.

The mountains, the sport, the new mountain railways and the Swiss expertise in hotel keeping resulted not only in a new holiday playground for the British but in a new and lucrative industry for Switzerland.

For those who preferred the colours of a Mediterranean landscape and long periods of warm sunshine, the French Riviera seemed the ideal venue for a holiday. Provence had had a great appeal for English visitors in the eighteenth century, for it lay on one of the routes to Italy and was itself rich in the classical remains which travellers of the eighteenth century vastly preferred to mountains. It was not until the second half of the nineteenth century that the opening up of new areas by the Continental railway system transformed the journey there from one of days to one of hours. From then on not only the leisured aristocracy but the busy middle classes were tempted southwards to the Mediterranean sunshine. Insignificant towns like Cannes and Nice grew and flourished in a new found prosperity. The impoverished principality of Monaco, because of its independent status, was able to offer the diversion of gambling to its visitors, and many Victorian gentlemen and ladies too were delighted to depart from their usual decorous behaviour and enjoy the excitement of an evening in the efficiently organized casino.

Cook's Tours

Many middle-class visitors to Switzerland and the Riviera were delighted to travel under the protection of Thomas Cook's flourishing travel organization. Encouraged by the success of his methods particularly during the Great Exhibition, when 165,000 excursionists from Yorkshire alone took advantage of his cheap fares, he decided to try a riskier enterprise, and for the Paris exhibition of 1855 he organised his first Continental tour. In 1865 he gave up all his other work, set up an office in London, and after a slow start became the model for all other subsequent travel agencies. Thomas Cook's success is a striking example of a service being offered to the right public at the right time. At this stage in the century clerks and shopkeepers as well as businessmen had more money to spare and their curiosity about other countries was reinforced by their longing to get away as far as possible from their uninspiring surroundings. Cook's tours were increasingly to satisfy this ambition, and at the same time to sustain their clients through any difficulties they might find in confronting foreign ways of speech and behaviour. To any critics who found this new institution of group travel somewhat vulgar, Mr Cook roundly replied, 'Let me ask why susceptibilities should be

46  An early excursion to see the splendours of Paris.

47 A choice of holiday, 1885.

48 A Victorian hostess dispenses tea to her party guests.

outraged, refinement trampled on, because thirty or forty Englishmen and Englishwomen find it convenient to travel on the same train, to coalesce for mutal benefit, to sojourn for a time in the same cities'.

The House Party

The upper classes, intrigued as they were by the delights of foreign travel, still enjoyed their own English countryside and spent much of their leisure time in one another's country houses. The custom grew throughout the Victorian age for groups of friends to gather together for a few days' shooting or for shorter Saturday to Monday stays, when they were able to enjoy many of the recognised pleasures of a holiday – change of scene, excellent and congenial company among some of the most beautifully planned gardens and parkland, the lushest countryside in Europe. During the Edwardian age this highly exclusive form of holiday had reached its peak of luxury and sophistication. King Edward VII himself whose taste for the company of amusing men and beautiful women was well known was a frequent and appreciative guest at the great houses of his most exalted and prosperous subjects.

The house party guests arrived by train, sometimes travelling in a private coach chartered by their host, and often the train would be specially halted at the nearest small station. They were met by a number of carriages for they brought vast quantities of luggage as well as their own personal maids and valets. Not for them the small weekend case of a later age, for part of the established ritual of these affairs was a constant changing of outfit. Lady Cynthia Asquith who though unquestionably well bred was not among the wealthiest members of Edwardian society, recalled in her book of memoirs the wardrobe that was considered indispensable even for a short visit. 'Two tweed coats and skirts with appropriate shirts, three evening frocks, three garments suitable for tea, your best hat – probably a vast affair loaded with feathers, flowers, fruit or corn – a variety of country hats and caps, . . . a riding habit, indoor and outdoor shoes, boots and gaiters . . . petticoats, shawls, scarves, ornamental combs and wreaths, and a large bag in which to carry your embroidery about the house'.

On arrival at the house the guests were allotted rooms with their names marked on the door, and due provision was made for the accompanying servants. The servants of the house were constantly busy keeping bedroom fires alight, carrying water for baths and helping to serve and prepare elaborate meals. Those meals, elaborate and prolonged, demonstrate more than anything else the plethora of servants on which the successful hostess depended. Breakfast consisted of an array of dishes laid on the sideboard from which the guests could help themselves to a large meal or a light snack. Lady Cynthia remembers 'lidded silver dishes where under little blue flames kept piping hot curly rashers of bacon; eggs poached,

49 Large hotels like this one in Scotland reproduce the pleasures of country house holidays.

fried or scrambled – mounds of moist kedgeree, haddocks afloat in melted butter, sizzling bursting sausages, ruddily exuding kidneys. . . . The finest trenchermen first lined themselves with porridge immersed in thick yellow cream and then piled on to their plate something out of practically every dish; After this they rammed down scones buttered two inches thick, and lavishly topped with marmalade, honey or home made jam. This third course was followed by fruit.' Lunch and dinner, more formal meals were even more varied and elaborate with numerous courses that had taken hours to prepare in well-staffed kitchens; they were served on tables lavishly decorated with flowers from the gardens and hothouses. For the guests with literary tastes there was of course the library; for the athletic there were the tennis courts, the croquet lawns and the grouse moors; and for the unashamedly frivolous – long hours of delicious gossip.

Although the country house holiday may seem of limited significance to a survey of the English holiday, it was ultimately to have a considerable influence on the development of the British hotel. As we have already seen, wherever the upper classes led, the middle classes were not slow to follow, and for them the country house hotel was to provide some of the attractions of the private houses of their wealthier countrymen. Country hotels were most determinedly based on the country house pattern, with their large staffs, their gardens, their chintz covered furniture and their tennis courts. They well suited the nineteenth-century middle class craving for the delights of nature among surroundings of the utmost comfort.

By the end of the nineteenth century, then, the concept of a holiday had been considerably enlarged and enriched. It no longer meant solely a day of traditional junketing, or a period spent away from home for the sake of improving one's health. The word 'holiday' had now acquired further shades of meaning. It became associated with beautiful surroundings, with the search for places that were new and exciting, with an interest in climbing and winter sports, and with leisurely relaxation among friends.

7 Between the Wars

The nineteenth century had been a time of transition in holiday making. The upper classes had begun to get used to the idea that a few weeks away from home each year was not only advisable for health reasons but was positively to be enjoyed. The working classes had accepted that their traditional holidays did not need to be spent at local fairs or on the village green – they could involve travel, fresh surroundings and new acquaintances.

It has also been a time of expansion. More areas had been opened up to tourists. Transport had improved and new holiday sports and pastimes had been developed.

The twentieth century was to see these developments continued until in our own time holidays have become sophisticated and varied to a degree that would have dazzled even the wealthiest and most adventurous of our Victorian forbears. Moreover this remarkable range of holidays has become available to a steadily increasing public.

50 The turn of the century. Seaside visitors were still elaborately dressed but there seems to have been a shift to more informal behaviour on the beach.

Holidays in the Country

The love of country life and delight in landscape that had begun to permeate British taste during the nineteenth century now became widespread. For clerks and factory workers horizons were broadening. They had begun to benefit from improved working conditions and the chance of a free education. Many young men and women were no longer content to endure the cramped and drab existence that had once seemed the inevitable lot of the industrial worker. As the labour movement struggled for greater political power and a more just and equitable society, many of its members worked to improve themselves and the quality of their lives. These people often turned their backs on the old working-class routine of a night at the pub, or even a day by the sea; they preferred to sling their rucksacks on their backs and head for the hills and the open country. The walking tour became popular with young men and women from the industrial cities as well as with undergraduates from more privileged backgrounds. And as the industrial towns expanded so the city dwellers turned to the pleasures of the countryside for rest and recreation.

In the early years of the century the walker or cyclist had to confine himself to day excursions or else take the risk of seedy lodgings or inns that were often too expensive for him at the end of the day. The solution to this problem was found first in Germany where by 1914 two hundred *Jugendherbergen* – Youth Inns – had been founded to cater for young people in search of an open air holiday. Many people in Britain were impressed by this development and there were various attempts to provide a similar network of overnight shelters for mountaineers and hikers. The most effective and enduring of these organisations was of course the Youth Hostels Association which is still today helping thousands of young people every year to enjoy a country holiday. The man who founded the association in 1930 – Jack Catchpool – was a man of energy as well as vision. He was supported

51 A transport poster advertises the delights of the country.

by the historian G. M. Treveleyan, who was himself a great country lover and the YHA's first president. By 1939 there were 297 hostels, concentrated in areas of outstanding interest and beauty. Sometimes they were set up in old farm houses or village schools; sometimes they were specially built. Wardens were appointed to supervise the hostels, and the accommodation was simple and communal but clean and reasonably comfortable. The young people were provided with a meal or allowed to cook their own food in a special kitchen. The night's stay in those early days cost them sixpence – a shilling if they were over eighteen – and they had to arrive at the hostel on foot or with a bicycle. The movement was, and still is, immensely successful. Parents who were doubtful about allowing their sons and daughters to roam about the countryside, uncertain of their destination, were reassured by the knowledge that their offspring were sure of food and a bed at the end of their day. For the first time a holiday was available that young people could feel had been specially designed for them, on which they could enjoy themselves in their own way, with their own contemporaries.

For those older people who preferred to make one place the centre of their walking holiday, and who wanted a reasonable standard of comfort, two other organisations – the Holiday Fellowship and the Cooperative Holidays Association were to prove invaluable. These were non-profit making bodies who took

52 Waterloo in 1906. Middle-class families returning from their long summer holidays.

over country properties and turned them into pleasant guest houses. Food was unprententious but good; walks and climbs ranging from the tough to the merely energetic were offered, and guests welcomed the chance of exploring the countryside with expert guides and congenial company.

The middle classes were coming to realize that holidays did not have to be spent by the sea. Not only were they beginning to patronise the large and comfortable country hotels which had so successfully emulated the ambience of Edwardian country house life; they were also beginning to buy or rent country cottages so that their families could spend their summer months entirely away from the towns. Bradford wool manufacturers with their families would migrate whenever possible to stone cottages in the Yorkshire Dales, business men in London would look for a quiet and pretty corner in the Home Counties. Artists and writers had their own favourite retreats among the South Downs, or in the as yet remote villages of Cornwall. Some families who could not afford to take servants on holiday with them and yet wanted to avoid domestic chores, spent their summer holidays on farms, where their children could enjoy the open air life which was so highly esteemed by middle-class parents, and where they could all enjoy excellent farmhouse food.

Whatever their social background, British people were beginning to regard the country as an alternative to the sea for their holidays. This was to have far reaching effects over the years on the pattern of rural life. Cottages originally built for farm workers acquired an entirely new value when they were seen as possible accommodation for summer tenants. Trade and services received a new stimulus, and the appearance of those villages popular with holiday visitors began to undergo subtle changes. Sometimes the changes were unfortunate – overhead telephone wires and garish advertising were inappropriate in places whose charm had lain in their old fashioned simplicity. On the other hand there were plenty of agricultural as well as industrial slums and a growing influx of visitors in search of the picturesque and the beautiful did something to make landlords more mindful of their responsibilities. Moreover, many of the town visitors were wealthy and their influence as well as their money went to support the societies dedicated to preserving the character of so many delightful villages.

This movement into the country was made possible not only by the growth of the railways with their increasingly complicated network of branch lines, but also by the development of the motor car. At first the invention of motor transport seemed to have little possible relevance to people of limited means. Apart from cheap railway excursions to the seaside or obvious beauty spots, they were still stuck firmly in the towns for the greater part of the year. Even a family picnic in woods or meadows on the outskirts of the big cities was difficult to arrange when there was no transport easily available. The motor car at first was too expensive to make any difference to this situation, but when the internal combustion engine which powered the motor was fitted to charabancs and omnibuses, life really began to open up. Ordinary people now had access to transport that was both

53 The advertising industry enters the holiday business.

cheap and easy to arrange. It was also immensely exciting. In his book *Cider With Rosie*, Laurie Lee conjures up for us something of the thrill of a trip in a motor charabanc. 'In our file of five charabancs', he records, 'a charioted army we swept down the thundering hills. At the speed and height of our vehicles the whole valley took on new dimensions; woods rushed beneath us, and fields and flies were devoured in a gulp of air. We were wind borne now by motion and pride, we cheered everything beast and fowl, and taunted with heavy ironical shouts those unfortunates still working in the fields.'

Although few people in Britain at the beginning of the century dreamed of ever owning their own private motor car, the adoption by British manufacturers of

54 The first Holiday Fellowship guest house at Newlands in the Lake District.

American techniques of mass production meant that small cheap cars came on to the British market. In 1910 there were less than 150,000 licensed motor vehicles on the roads of Britain; by 1939 there were over 3 million. A new influx of drivers uninhibited by driving tests took to the roads in their Fords, their baby Austins and their Morris Minors, and spent much of their leisure time not only in their cars but underneath them, as they grappled with novel and fascinating problems.

The adoption of motoring as a leisure pastime led to the formation of the two great motoring organizations – The Royal Automobile Club and The Automobile Association. These bodies in return for a yearly subscription from their members undertook, as they still do today, to provide a comprehensive service to the motorist. They were able to protect the interests of the motorist at government level and to offer breakdown services, maps, insurance and a list of hotels personally inspected by their officials.

Hotel Accommodation

This inspection of hotels provided by the AA and RAC was particularly useful in view of the unreliable standards of hotel keeping that prevailed throughout the country. As we have seen, the large expensive hotels had achieved high standards of comfort and service, but holiday makers of more modest means were often badly served. The old inns and coaching houses could be unsatisfactory and visitors in search of overnight accommodation were often dismayed by poor food and squalid bedrooms. The inspection and grading of hotels helped to remedy this. Businessmen too realized that a profitable future lay ahead for those hotels which could be relied on for comfort and efficiency, and they invested money and expertise in organizing chains of well run hotels. The best known of these enterprises was perhaps Trust Houses Ltd which bought a number of inns throughout Britain and refurbished and renewed the old traditions of comfort and good food.

Holidays With Pay

To those people living in the depressed industrial areas of Britain during the 1930s, the sight of some of their luckier countrymen jaunting about the country in their cars and staying at good hotels must have seemed a bitter contrast with their own miserable conditions. Yet, despite the Depression, there were every year more people who could afford a holiday, and whose employers were coming to accept a week's holiday with pay for their employees, as a regular institution. The Trade Unions adopted the idea of a guaranteed holiday as part of their general policy, and there was mounting criticism of the government's failure to introduce a compulsory annual holiday for all workers. However, despite prolonged investigations and many attempts at private members' bills in Parliament, the government only went so far as to recommend to employers that they should provide at least a week off every year for all their work people; there was no compulsion. Only in the case of agricultural workers and certain small and possibly vulnerable trades like hair dressing, button manufacturing and paper bag making, were government authorities set up to supervise their conditions of employment, including, of course, the provision of an annual holiday.

The Seaside Resorts

The majority of British people lucky enough to get a holiday from work and to have money to spare, still, in the period between the wars, joined in the summer rush to the sea. By the late thirties it was estimated that 15 million people each year were able to spend at least a week away from home and the seaside resorts did their best to make sure that they kept their boarding houses full and their promenades crowded. Blackpool was perhaps the most lavish of all in her expenditure on tourist attractions, with her miles of promenade, her illuminations and the spectacular Tower which loomed over miles of flat Lancashire landscape as a perpetual reminder of the delights of its ballroom and circus. Other resorts did their best with immaculately kept formal gardens, boating lakes, variety shows and concerts. Beaches were provided with public lavatories, deck chairs and wind breaks. Cafeterias, a new institution of the thirties, provided inexpensive snacks and beach trays for those who did not object to sand in their cups of tea. More-

55 Seaside towns needed long roads of boarding houses and hotels to accommodate their visitors.

over, the seaside holiday was now recognized by newspapers and the advertising industry as a great national pastime ripe for exploitation and therefore they did all they could to encourage it. Nationwide sand castle building competitions were organized, and the children of Britain aided and abetted by perspiring parents toiled over elaborate and flag bedecked fortifications. The *News Chronicle* organized the popular Lobby Ludd contests, during which a gentleman with this unlikely name toured the British resorts. His photograph was displayed in the current copies of the *News Chronicle*, and any holidaymaker who recognized him as he strolled along the beach was invited to confront him armed, of course, with that day's issue of the newspaper, and to challenge him with the words, 'You are Lobby Ludd and I claim the *News Chronicle* prize.'

Factories in Birmingham and Sheffield and, of course, Hong Kong made the most of this new opportunity and produced a range of souvenirs, toys and sweets specially designed to tempt seaside visitors. Monogrammed mugs, sugar spoons and biscuit barrels decorated mantel pieces and sideboards all over Britain. Children's seaside holidays were given special savour by the sweets stocked by seaside booths and stalls – candy floss, enormous sticks of rock and extra large and lurid ice creams. The children also knew the delights of a plethora of special

56 Billy Butlin's first holiday camp at Skegness in 1937.

57 Thomas Cook and Son went on extending their range of holidays.

seaside toys – buckets and spades, packets of flags for flying from the top of sand castles, yo-yos, hi-li bats, small intriguing tins for moulding sand patterns and perhaps best of all the surprise packets, in which could be found a whole series of delights, from chewing gum to small pieces of rock that when dropped in water magically blossomed into little magic underwater gardens.

Holiday Camps

In 1937 there appeared an entirely new version of the seaside holiday; Billy Butlin opened his first holiday camp at Skegness. Mr Butlin had made a fortune from running a spectacular fairground in Canada and came to Britain, the original home of his parents, with money to invest. Besides money he also had the intelligence to reach two important conclusions. First, he perceived that for most people a holiday was a major expense, and that therefore they would welcome with relief the chance of a holiday offered at an all-in price with no unexpected charges. He also realised that many people did not want a holiday of total inactivity – they often preferred to be organized, even dragooned into recreations and into meeting new people. His diagnosis was dead accurate, and his new venture became popular and profitable.

Holidays Abroad

An increasing number of people had the money and the ambition to venture farther afield. For them the travel organizations provided an increasing variety of foreign tours. Prices fell considerably as more and more agencies chartered continental trains for their clients. There was also the chance to go on inexpensive cruises, as many of the big shipping lines, hard hit by the Depression, turned their attention to organizing short cruises in the sunshine. Yet again a holiday once thought to be the exclusive preserve of the rich was opened up to the public, and they responded with enthusiasm. For as little as six guineas they could take a six-day cruise to Norway, and for just over £3 a weekend trip along the coasts of Northern France, Belgium and Holland, with shipboard entertainments and sightseeing excursions included in the price.

European countries were beginning to understand the boost to their economies that could result from a flourishing tourist trade. Their catering and transport services, their hotels and pensions were increasingly geared to attract the foreign visitor. Tourist offices representing most European countries were established in London with posters and brochures made available with which to attract British visitors. Their success and that of the travel agencies that were flourishing even in the smallest towns, pointed to the growing assumption that the continent of Europe was now an easy place to get to and that foreign holidays would become more commonplace every year. It was an assumption that was to be eroded by the mounting tensions between Nazi Germany and her neighbours and to be finally dispelled by the outbreak of the Second World War in September 1939.

8 Holidays Today

During the Second World War, the British holiday industry shut down. All the country's energies and resources were applied to the war effort. Servicemen were billeted in the boarding houses and drilled along the promenades. Barbed wire and tank traps formed a line of defence along the sea shores; paint work peeled off the once elegant hotels and the public gardens were covered with weeds. A railway system that was constantly on the alert for the transport of troops could not afford to be choked with crowds of civilian holiday makers. The government urged that everyone should take their holidays at home. Indeed there was not much incentive to travel when there were so few places to stay; when one's route might lie through areas liable to be bombed; and when the sea even when it was accessible was full of mines. Most people, when they snatched a holiday during the war, visited relatives living in the safer parts of the country, or visited quiet country pubs. There was little chance of taking an occasional trip in a car, for petrol was rationed with increasing stringency.

58 August Bank Holiday, 1944.

59 Cheaper air fares have brought transatlantic holidays within reach of a wider public.

Holidays Begin Again

Once the war was over, the long period of restriction seemed to have sharpened everyone's desire for a holiday. Britain's balance of payments position had been considerably weakened by the demands made on her economy by her five years of fighting. For several years after the war, anyone leaving the country on holiday was only allowed to take thirty-five pounds' worth of foreign currency. Yet, ironically, never had there been so many people who could afford to spend money on foreign travel. The war had seen a considerable rise in wages, and many workers had been able to save reasonable amounts from their overtime pay. At a time when there was still little to buy in post-war Britain, and when rationing was still in force, a trip to a prosperous, well-stocked country like Switzerland attracted many people abroad for the first time.

Air Travel

By this time a new dimension had been added to holiday travel with the expansion of the air services. Before the war air travel had been generally regarded as an interesting phenomenon but not as a way of travel that ordinary people would ever use. To the public at large it had seemed exotic but unreliable not to say dangerous. How different was the picture by the late 1940s when British people had become accustomed to young men quartering the skies in their insubstantial looking Spitfires and Hurricanes and to large aircraft flying long distances every night to bomb German towns, and to diplomats and statesmen using the air as their highway. After the war the application of the jet engine to passenger planes opened up the possibility of speedy inter-continental flights in large comfortable aircraft. The travel agencies were able to take advantage of fare concessions by the airlines and to wrap up attractive package holidays including air fares and hotel accommodation for a price little more than the cost of an ordinary flight. Once again the public interested in foreign holidays was increased, for people who grudged spending two days of their precious fortnight's holiday sitting on a train, felt quite differently about a two-hour flight to the sunshine. Spain, Portugal, Majorca even North Africa were now within comfortable reach, and within the pockets of many people whose grandparents had considered a journey of fifty miles a major adventure.

The sixties saw a new phenomenon in air travel – the growth of charter flights. The price of air fares is fixed by an international body – the International Air Transport Association – to which all the world's airlines belong. This association has drawn up agreements to fix prices and so to avoid unnecessary price cutting. However the IATA agreements allowed airlines to make considerable reductions in fares if a genuine association of people (a sports club or music society, for instance) chartered a plane exclusively for their members. There was an additional proviso that the members should have belonged to the club for at least six months. This arrangement was of obvious benefit to the passengers, and the airlines were pleased to get a full pay load of passengers to fly at the off peak times when they usually found difficulty in filling their normal scheduled flights. This arrangement was to become a backdoor for organizations specializing in cheap charter flights. It was easy enough to bend the rules a little and many people crossed the Atlantic and even the Pacific carrying membership cards of quickly formed clubs that they had in fact only joined a few days before their journey. There were occasional unfortunate scenes when Ministry of Transport Inspectors, having been tipped off that a certain charter flight was not carrying *bona fide* club members, descended on the plane ready on the tarmac, and forbade the flight. In spite of these occasional misfortunes the charter system, both official and unofficial, flourished; it became a simple matter to pick out an agency from the back page of *The Times* and fix up a flight to Toronto or Sydney at a few days notice. In the end the airlines themselves were allowed to offer cheap long distance flights to passengers who were willing to book their journeys some months ahead and to travel during off peak periods. 'Earthshrinking flights' can now be openly advertised.

A Variety of Choice
Cheap air fares, whether official or unofficial have brought the destination of the mediaeval pilgrim and eighteenth-century aristocrat within the reach of many thousands of people. Holiday-makers can now enjoy the experiences and sights

60 Skiers often form a small party.

enjoyed by Brother Fabri in the Holy Land after a flight lasting only a few hours. Millions of ordinary people have been able to enjoy the architectural splendours of Italy which once only the rich could afford to visit. For those prepared to spend three or four hundred pounds on a holiday even more exciting opportunities have been opened up. One specialist travel agency offers a flight to Venice, followed by a cruise in the Mediterranean or Aegean Sea with guest lecturers to give the background for visits to famous archaeological sites like Mycenae or Delphi. The same organization offers tours of India, Persia, Mexico or Ethiopia. Sights which were once reserved for explorers are now open to those with money to spend.

Winter sports have ceased to be the privilege of the wealthy. Even in the years immediately after the war when travellers could only get to the ski slopes by long and exhausting train journey, thousands of people managed to get equipment together and escaped from an austere Britain to the winter sun. As the travel agencies moved in on this profitable scene, the packages became even more attractive to the novice as well as the expert, for they could buy, in the inclusive price, a course of instruction and hire of skis.

Wealthy people whose taste was for adventure in the sun rather than in the snow could if they chose go to Africa on safari. They could join parties accompanied, of course, by guides and explore the game reserves of Kenya, Uganda and Tanzania.

Many people travelling abroad preferred to organize their own itineraries, particularly if they were taking their own car. The AA and RAC found themselves increasingly busy as more and more motorists crossed the channel and took advantage of their route planning and insurance services. Particularly valuable and reassuring were the facilities for medical insurance, for few foreign countries have reciprocal agreements with Britain for free medical treatment, and many tourists have been embarrassed by the misfortune and expense of falling ill while on holiday.

As the choice of locale for foreign holidays has widened so also has the range of

61 Cars, camping equipment and caravans give families wider opportunities to travel.

accommodation. Travellers are no longer limited to hotels and pensions. More and more people are renting their own holiday houses, sometimes privately, sometimes through agencies specialising in holiday rentals. These offer houses and chalets, often with maid service included in the rent, as a separate arrangement with the client or as a package deal with air fare included in the price of the holiday. For those who find life in a large hotel somewhat impersonal, there are chalet parties, where one can join a small group of people in an informal atmosphere.

A widely used extension to the scope of foreign holidays has been the development of camping. The introduction of the frame tent has revolutionised the whole ideas of spending a holiday under canvas. Many families set off for the Continent every year carrying their accommodation on the roof of their car, and having found a camp site put up a tent in which they can stand upright, and which has separate rooms. Camping equipment too has become more sophisticated. Air beds are comfortable and quick to put up with electric pumps; cookers though light to carry can cope with substantial meals; and the insulated ice box means that the camper can store his food and also luxuriate in the sound of ice clinking in the glass of his evening drink. The camper has the choice of staying in the wilds or visiting one of the top grade camp sites with their hot showers, camp shops and restaurants.

Holidays for the Young
Today when our student population is steadily increasing many young people choose to spend working holidays. Many fruit farms who once welcomed pickers from London's East End, now employ students of all nationalities, and provide them with adequate if spartan accommodation. These fruit picking holidays

provide an opportunity to meet young people from all over the world as well as for earning pocket money. The more adventurous can find farm work abroad, and enjoy helping with the grape harvest in France. Many have been able to visit Israel and have the exciting experience of working on a kibbutz.

The National Union of Students has had, since the war, a special travel department organizing holidays at the cheapest possible rates. Many of their earliest charter flights after the war used somewhat primitive aircraft, but nevertheless with limited resources they managed to offer a remarkably wide range of holiday destinations. Their services now of course are even more comprehensive and considerably more sophisticated.

For young people of all ages who like an open air holiday all sort of possibilities are available. The Outward Bound Trust organize holidays during the Summer for boys and girls who like to match themselves against difficult conditions. They are taken under skilled supervision on mountaineering and canoeing expeditions and taught the crafts necessary to survival in open country.

Organizations like the National Council for Physical Recreation offer holiday courses designed to teach specific skills. Holiday courses are available at centres devoted to various sports – pony trekking, sailing, rock climbing, tennis or canoeing.

62 This youth hostel at Longthwaite in Borrowdale was especially built as a hostel.

63 Pony trekking is a favourite activity especially for young people.

Although there is as yet in Britain no full scale provision of holidays for young children, as there is in France and the United States, there are signs of a dawning response to demands for an occasional holiday away from their parents. The Scouts and Guides have been pioneers in this field, and many schools, encouraged by their success, now organize school trips during the summer term. The parties either stay in accommodation provided by their local education authorities or take over hotels at cheap out of season rates. For those pupils who can afford them, many schools also offer foreign holidays during the Summer and Easter breaks. Many young people join school cruises to Scandinavia or the Mediterranean, and the popularity of school Winter Sports parties is demonstrated by the crowds of school children congregating at Victoria station during the Christmas and Easter holidays.

For those wishing to stay in their own country and who take an interest in the arts, there are summer courses in drama and music organized by education authorities and by groups anxious to encourage the enthusiasm of young people for the arts.

Special Interest Holidays

Grown-ups as well as children often enjoy spending their holiday at a Summer School either following their special hobbies or developing new enthusiasms. Some universities and colleges find Summer Schools a useful way of filling their

64 The National Council for Physical Recreation arranges a wide variety of holiday courses every summer.

empty dining halls and lecture rooms during the vacation, and some like Loughborough have embarked on the interesting experiment of providing family-centred courses. Mothers and fathers can enjoy their psychology or music courses in peace while their children occupy themselves in the workshops and art rooms.

There are other opportunities, apart from the Summer Schools, to spend holidays centred on the Arts. The Shakespeare Festival at Stratford-on-Avon offers the chance of combining a visit to the theatre to see The Royal Shakespeare Company with the delights of the Cotswolds. The Edinburgh Festival and the Bath Festival provide superb concerts in cities that are themselves fascinating places for a holiday. The annual festival organized by Benjamin Britten at Aldeburgh gives visitors a musical holiday whose pleasures are sharpened by a tang of the sea.

The Problems

Like all pastimes indulged in by an ever increasing population, holiday making presents us with problems as well as pleasures. Just as the motor car and the jet plane can pollute our atmosphere, unrestricted holiday development can despoil our coastline and countryside. Cheap travel has meant that most of us at some time get the chance of a Mediterranean holiday, but it has also brought polluted

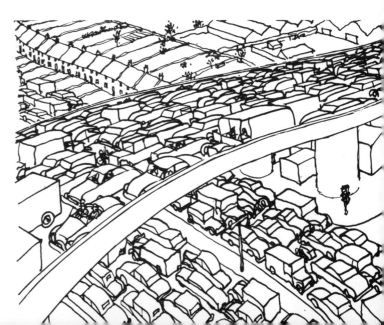

65 'So this is a traffic jam.'

beaches and ugly hotel development to a coastline that was once the most beautiful in the world. The chance of a seaside holiday for everyone is fine but we must take care not to repeat the mistakes made in Sussex, where miles of beautiful coastal scenery have been spoiled either by sprawling developments of bungalows or badly sited industries. Pleasure that Cornwall is now accessible to thousands of visitors is somewhat tarnished by the thought of the traffic queues along the Exeter by-pass and of the crowds packed tight in the rocky coves and fishing villages. The setting aside of certain areas as National Parks, the planning of picnic areas, the work of the National Trust all help to keep some of the worst effects of our enthusiasm for holidays from the places where we most like to take them.

Whatever the future holds, it seems certain that the people of Britain are unlikely to relinquish their hard won right to a yearly break from routine. They will go on somehow finding their way to the mountains, or to the sun. Their children will see to it that donkeys, ice cream stalls, and sand castles remain an honoured and inviolate part of their holiday landscape.

Books for Further Reading
H. S. Bennett, *Life on the Mediaeval Manor*.
Miles and John Hadfield, *The English Christmas*.
R. J. Mitchell and M. D. R. Leys, *A History of London Life*.
Alan Kendall, *Mediaeval Pilgrims*.
H. F. M. Prescott, *Jerusalem Journey*.
Zoe Oldenbourg, *The World is not Enough*.
Jane Austen, *Northanger Abbey*.
        Persuasion.
John Walters, *Splendour and Scandal*.
Edith Sitwell, *Bath*.
Georgette Heyer, *Bath Tangle*.
        The Black Sheep.
Tobias Smollet, *Humphry Clinker*.
Ruth Manning Sanders, *Seaside England*.
Pimlott, *Englishman's Holiday*.
Hern, *The English Seaside Holiday*.
Laurie Lee, *Cider with Rosie*.
Flora Thompson, *Lark Rise to Candleford*.
J. B. Priestley, *English Journey*.
        The Edwardians.
Clifford Musgrave, *Brighton*.
Perkin, *The Age of the Railway*.

Index

Numerals in **bold type** refer to pages on which illustrations appear.

Ales, in mediaeval times, 13
Alpine Club, The, 69
Alpine Climbing, 69
Anglo Saxons, 8
Arnold, Dr Thomas, 53
Asquith, Lady Cynthia, 74
Austen, Jane, 66
Automobile Association, 81
Avebury, **18**, 19

Balmoral, 67, **67**
Bank Holiday Act, 60
Bath, **34**, **35**, **39**
    As a watering place, 30
    Routine at, 31
    Effect of Beau Nash on, 33
bathing machines, 42
bathing wear, 44, 56, **57**, 58
Beale, Benjamin, 44
Blackpool, 82
Bournemouth, 62
Breydenbach, Bernard Von, 28
Bridlington, 66
Brighton, 47, 49, 60, 62
Brönte, Anne, 66
Brönte, Charlotte, 66
Burney, Fanny, 46
Butlin, Billy, 85

camping holidays, 90, **90**
Catherine of Braganza, 30
chalet parties, 90
charabancs, 79
charter flights, 88
Chaucer, 26
Christianity, 8
Christmas, in the Middle Ages, 10, 11
church, in the Middle Ages, 10
Clarke, Rev. William, 65
Cook, Thomas, 71, 72

Cooks Tours, **71**, **72**
Cooperative Holidays Association, 78
corn dollies, 10
Cornwall, 44
country houses, 73, 74
cruises, 85

dancing, in mediaeval times, 14
Deal, 52
Defoe, Daniel, 36
Depression, The, 82
dippers, 43

Earthshrinker flights, **87**, 88
Easter, 10, 11
Edward VII, King, 73
Exhibition, The Great (1851), 61

Fabri, Brother Felix, 20
fairs, in mediaeval times, 17
Farrow, Mrs, 40
feasts, in mediaeval times, 11
Floyer, Sir John, 41
foreign travel, 68, 71, 85
football, 13
Freya, the Goddess, 8

games, in the Middle Ages, 13
George III, King, 46, 47
Glastonbury, 9, **9**
Grand Tour, 37, 38
    Its effect on design, 39
Gunn, Martha, 43

harvest suppers, 12
health, the search for, 69
holiday camps, 85
Holiday Fellowship, the, 78, **81**
holidays,
    In earlier times, 7
    Roman, 8

Anglo Saxon, 8
   Effects of Christianity on, 9
   In the Middle Ages, 10
   Connection with farming year, 12
   Games, 13
   Cottages for, 79
   By the sea, 82
   Package holidays, 88
   With lectures, 89
   For health reasons, 30
   At spas, 35
   At the sea, 40, 82
   Effects of railways on, 52
   In Victorian times, 54
   For the working classes, 59
   For poor children, 64
   In the country, 73
   In Edwardian times, 74
   Winter, 89
   In Africa, 89
   Camping, 90
   For the young, 90
Hoys, Margate, 43

Industrial Revolution,
   Effects of transport, 58, 59
   Effects of British way of life, 58
International Air Transport Association, 85
India, tours to, 89

Jerusalem, 19, 24, 26, 27, **27**
jousting, 4

Knights of Malta, 22
Knights Templar, 23

Lamb, Charles, 45
landscape, painting, 65
Lee, Laurie, 80

Margate, 43, 45
mass production,
   Its effect on availability, 43, 45
   Of motor cars,
Man, Isle of, 52
May festivals, 9
Mediaeval Church, the, 10
Mellitus, Archbishop, 9
Midwinter festivals, 8, 9, **16**
middle-class holidays, 53, **55**, 71
mineral waters, 30
miracle plays, 14
Misrule, Lord of, 11
motor car, 81
mountaineering, 69
mummers, **12**
mumming plays, 14

Nash, John, 49
Nash, Richard, 32, 33, 34
National Council of Physical Recreation, 91, **93**
national parks, 94

National Union of Students, 91

Old Smoaker, dipper to the Prince Regent, 43
Outward Bound Trust, 91

Pavilion, Brighton, **48**, 49
package holidays, 88
pagan festivals, 7, 8, 9
Pepys, Samuel, 31
Picaud, Aimery, 21
pilgrim galleys, 24
pilgrimages, **10**, 18–21, 23
pilgrims, 20, 22–24, **25**, 27
pony trekking, **92**
Pope, Gregory, 8
Prince Regent, The, 39, 43

railways, 53
religious festivals, 7–10
resorts, by the sea, 49, 51
Riviera, The, 70, **70**
Rogation Tide, 11
Romans, The, 8
Royal Automobile Club, The, 81

safari, holidays, 89
Santiago de Compostela, 21
Scarborough, 41, **43**, 55
Scotland, 67
sea bathing, 40, 42, 55
Seaford, **53**
seaside holidays, origin of, 40
seaside resorts, 44
Second World War, 85, 86
Shrove Tuesday, 10
Smollet, Tobias, 31
spas, origin of, 29
steam power, 52
summer schools, 92
Switzerland, 68, 69, 70

tollgates, **51**
topsy-turvydom in mediaeval festivals, 11
toys, on holiday, 85
transport, development of, 4, 9
Treveleyan, G. M., 78
Trust Houses, 82
Tunbridge Wells, **30**, 30
turnpikes, 49, **50**

Venice, 22
Victoria, Queen, 67
village life, 79

Wakes Weeks, 59, 63
Weymouth, 46, 47, **47**
Wittie, Robert, 31
winter sports, 89
working-class holidays, 58, 59, 63

Youth Hostels Association, 78, 79
Yule, 9